Lucia Posey
LIFE Worthy of Life:
Voices of Descendants of Euthanasia Victims

Lucia Posey

LIFE Worthy of Life:
Voices of Descendants of Euthanasia Victims

Umschlagabbildung: 'Connecting', mixed media collage, Sarva Lucia Posey

This work is a dissertation submitted to the Faculty of the European Graduate School, Division Expressive Arts Therapy, Education, Consulting, in Candidacy for the Degree of Doctor of Philosophy in March 2012.

ISBN 978-3-86596-518-9

© Frank & Timme GmbH Verlag für wissenschaftliche Literatur
Berlin 2013. Alle Rechte vorbehalten.

Das Werk einschließlich aller Teile ist urheberrechtlich geschützt. Jede Verwertung außerhalb der engen Grenzen des Urheberrechtsgesetzes ist ohne Zustimmung des Verlags unzulässig und strafbar. Das gilt insbesondere für Vervielfältigungen, Übersetzungen, Mikroverfilmungen und die Einspeicherung und Verarbeitung in elektronischen Systemen.

Herstellung durch das atelier eilenberger, Taucha bei Leipzig.
Printed in Germany.
Gedruckt auf säurefreiem, alterungsbeständigem Papier.

www.frank-timme.de

To the victims of the Nazi regime's program of Euthanasia
and descendants of those victims

Acknowledgements

First, thank you to the participants of this study for their willingness to allow me to take part in their lives. I am encouraged by the way each one overcomes life's adversity.

Thank you to my dissertation advisors, Sally Atkins Ed.D. and Kelly Clark/Keefe Ed.D., for supporting me in this dissertation journey.

Thank you to my editors, Janet Salas and Jane Johansen PhD for helping me climb the mountain of "writing scientific English," Dr. Beate Ringwelski, for her encouragement and her analytical mind, and Ralf Dantscher, for his unwavering walking by my side and emotional support. I thank Dr. Herbert Eberhart for his reflective feedback on the methodology section of the dissertation and Francine Guibentif for reading and reflecting the text and for our artistic work together. Thank you to my family and friends who have provided encouragement, support, and food for the body and soul.

Thank you too, to Dr. Georg Lilienthal, *Gedenkstätte Hadamar*, for his early support of this study and to the *Arbeitskreis zur Erforschung der Euthanasie* for keeping the memories of the victims alive.

Table of Contents

Acknowledgements — 7

1.0 INTRODUCTION — 13
  1.1 Limitations — 13
  1.2 Research Historical Background — 13
  1.3 Research Purpose — 14
  1.4 Research Focus — 15
  1.5 The Research Questions — 15
  1.6 Significance of Study — 15
  1.7 Methodology — 16
  1.8 The Design and Organisation of the Dissertation — 16
  1.9 Research Impact — 16
  1.10 Definitions of Special Terms — 17
  1.11 Conceptual Foundations — 18

2.0 CONCEPTUAL CONTEXT — 19
  2.1 History of Crimes — 19
    2.1.1 Literature on the Descendants of the Euthanasia and Holocaust Victims — 21
    2.1.2 Literature on Intrapsychic Effects of the Nazi Regime — 22
    2.1.3 Literature on Shame — 24
    2.1.4 Literature on the Descendants of the Perpetrators — 25

    2.2 Personal Context   25
- 2.2.1 Bias and Subjectivity   26
- 2.2.2 Language, Language Barriers and Voices   27
- 2.2.3 Meetings with Differently-abled People   28

    2.3 Summary   30

3.0 METHODOLOGICAL FRAMEWORK AND RESEARCH DESIGN   31

    3.1 Methodology   32
- 3.1.1 Qualitative Research   32
- 3.1.2 Autoethnography and Ethnography   33
- 3.1.3 Post-qualitative: Decentering and Arts-Based Research   33

    3.2 Research Design   34
- 3.2.1 Qualitative Narrative Inquiry   35
- 3.2.2 Arts-Based Collective Case Study   35

    3.3 Interview   38
- 3.3.1 Decentering   40
- 3.3.2 Aesthetic Preliminary Analysis   40
- 3.3.3 Harvesting   41
- 3.3.4 Thematic Data Analysis   42

    3.4 Subjectivity   43

4.0 FINDINGS   45

    4.1 Victims of Euthanasia during the Nazi Regime   45

    4.2 Portraits of the Participants   50

    4.3 Summary of the Findings, Emerging Themes   58
- 4.3.1 Passing on the Intergenerational Trauma   58
- 4.3.2 Present Day Quality of Life   69
- 4.3.3 Impact of the Decentering on the Responses to the Interview Questions   74
- 4.3.4 Conclusions on Using Decentering as a Research Method   92
- 4.3.5 Role of the Researcher   93
- 4.3.6 Conclusion of the Findings: Life Worthy of Life   100

5.0 RECOMMENDATIONS FOR FURTHER RESEARCH		102
5.1	Implications of This Study	102
5.2	Suggestions for Further Research	102
5.3	Further Aspirations	103
6.0 WORKS CITED		106
7.0 APPENDIX		109
7.1	Lay Summary	109
7.2	A Dialog between Anna and Lucy	110

1.0 INTRODUCTION

This study is built on a life-defining experience as a descendant of a Euthanasia victim. The following chapters are an attempt to represent the stories of other descendants in the same life situation and to establish the extent of the influence of this life experience in both the individuals and their society using expressive arts.

1.1 Limitations

At the beginning of my research, I contacted the memorial sites of the towns of Hadamar and Grafeneck. "The descendants are very shy," Dr. Lilienthal, Director of the Center for Social Psychiatry in Hadamar, wrote in a letter when I asked for support in finding participants for this study. He was quite discouraging about this project and wrote in an email on October 6, 2008, that he acknowledged the difficult task. He continued that the knowledge about the victims was hidden for many decades until it was forgotten. What is remembered is difficult for family members to talk about and share with a third party.

Being a part of the group I was researching, I took all my courage and continued with the project. The descendants have a right to have their stories told, and my intuition told me that the descendants' lives had possibly been influenced by the murder of their relative.

1.2 Research Historical Background

Euthanasia in the context of this study refers to this crime as committed by the Nazi regime. As Richter formulates it—the killing of so-called life unworthy of life is aimed against the mentally disabled and chronically psychiatric patients and groups of people who are undesirable (22). The extent of the crimes is still being discovered today. As recent as January 2011, mass graves with 200 bodies were unearthed near the psychiatric hospital in the town of Hall, Austria.

Killing the disadvantaged and disabled people for the reason of purifying the German race (Klee 18) was the beginning of the Holocaust in Nazi Germany. When the National Socialist party came to power in 1933, its members implemented orders to kill people who did not fit the picture, the *Menschenbild* of a healthy and productive citizen. The killings were supposedly intended to further the Germanic race both through the elimination of hereditary diseases and the eradication of people who did not fit into a society of Aryan superiority. This included long-term patients of psychiatric hospitals, homeless people, prostitutes, homosexuals, traumatized World War I soldiers, and prisoners of war. The victims of the Euthanasia crimes were seen as "empty human shells" about whom could be said, "Their death will not leave the smallest gap" (Binding/Hoche 30). First were the long-term patients of the psychiatric hospitals selected to be killed in the gas chambers. Those carrying out the killings implemented what Binding and Hoche termed a *policy of mercy killing* (36). In his book, *The Nazi Doctors*, Lifton quotes Hoche who postulated that a way to strengthen the country after a devastating defeat in the World War I was to eliminate "life not worth living": The state organism ... with its own laws and rights, much like a self-contained human organism ... which, in the interest of the welfare of the whole, also—as we doctors know—abandons and rejects parts or particles that have become worthless or dangerous" (45).

This *scientific racism* had already been discussed in German intellectual circles in the last decade of the 19th century. The German people, who on some level believed the propaganda which had started before the National Socialist party came to power, killed the victims in spirit. By believing the state has the power over life and death they believed any human being who does not fit the norm is not worth living (Lifton 46). The new Nazi regime adopted these ideas in order to eliminate any unwanted persons through murder and prevention of bearing and procreating children.

After the killings of the Euthanasia victims in the gas chambers was officially stopped, however, the killings continued through injections, overdoses of medication, and starvation. The Euthanasia murders in the gas chambers of the psychiatric hospitals preceded the killings in the concentration camps.

When researching the lives of the descendants, at times rage and shame about what people can do to each other overshadowed my research into the lives of the participants. Klee writes in the introduction to his book *"Euthanasie" im NS-Staat* [*Euthanasia during the Nazi regime*] about his process of researching the Euthanasia crimes. He felt this shame and rage in relation to the crimes committed. He had to correct himself several times, as rage and shame are not easily suppressed (11).

1.3 Research Purpose

The purpose of this research is to identify and trace the effects of the Nazi Euthanasia practices during World War II on the descendants of the victims during a time when their families' collective memory still holds traces of details of the victims, their lives, and their deaths. The purpose of this study is also to observe and substantiate the effects of expressive arts in interviews about emotionally sensitive stories told by the participants.

1.4 Research Focus

In this dissertation, the stories of the second- and third-generation descendants of Euthanasia victims are told. This study explores how descendants' lives are shaped by their personal story and the effects of this intergenerational trauma on the family structures (Bar-On, *Die Last des Schweigens, Hoffnung bis zu den Enkeln des Holocaust*). The research is also focused on using the arts as means to explore possible underlying issues.

1.5 The Research Questions

This study looks at the way this population makes meaning of their lives, cares for and grieves for their loved ones, and how the descendants turn toward and away from the unspoken in their families. The study researches how art added richness and complexity to the interviews and to the research process as a whole.

This study examines how the trauma of having a disabled relative who was also a Euthanasia victim is passed on to the next generations and how shame prevents the secret to be uncovered. The study examines if this wall of shame can be broken and the family secret revealed without passing on the shame to the next generation.

The research explored the way descendants of Euthanasia victims make meaning of their lives, care for and grieve for their loved one, and how the descendants turn towards and away from the unspoken in the family.

An additional research question examined the use of art-making with decentering during the interview. The study further explored how art-making in data collection, analysis and presentation added richness and complexity to the interviews and to the research process as a whole.

As an aspect of qualitative and autoethnographic research, the subjective view of the researcher is an important influence in the study. Through ongoing self-reflective writing and art-making, I sought to intensify my awareness of my complex subjectivities throughout this study.

1.6 Significance of Study

Having a disabled Euthanasia victim in a family also shapes family members' lives today. This study is an attempt to show how family lives encounter the influence of having a disabled relative who was murdered. It is also significant that no dissertation or other extensive research had been done about this population at the time when this dissertation research began: Previously the issue of shame seems to overshadowed the possibility of research.

The issue of Euthanasia is still current today. Forced sterilizations on physically and mentally disabled people are executed yet today. Euthanasia on old and incurably ill people, assisted suicide, and pre-implantation diagnoses is widely practiced.

1.7 Methodology

The research is a qualitative arts based multiple case study. For this qualitative study, six participants were interviewed. Narrative inquiry techniques as well as arts based methods including prose, poetry, and drawings were used as research methods throughout the study. Decentering based on Knill's method of decentering in the therapeutic process was used in the interviews to expand the issues and deepen the results through art-making.

1.8 The Design and Organisation of the Dissertation

The background of the study is provided by the literature of the Euthanasia crimes and the Holocaust. The study is based on the researcher's, the participants', and published authors' passion for and dedication into the research of the Holocaust and the Euthanasia crimes. The literature review supports the emerging themes of intergenerational trauma and shame.

The third chapter speaks about the methodological framework and research design. The methodology is the framework which carries and organizes the findings and connects it to the conceptual context. This methodology consists of qualitative and post-qualitative inquiry, which provides an epistemological theory to this study.

The findings report what I learned from the stories and the themes that emerged from the interviews, art-making, field logs, diaries, and publications. The art-making during the interview added to the interview, triggered memories, and inspired emotionally laden responses adding richness and complexity to the stories told. Included in this study are subjective elements and thoughts marked by italicized paragraphs.

The participants in this study all speak German, and all interviews were conducted in German. I translate their words here in all instances. I also provide translations of book titles and occasional names of places.

1.9 Research Impact

I intend to contribute to the field of expressive arts by using the method of decentering with art-making during the interviews. My intention is to contribute to research depth on the result of Nazi crimes in the lives of the descendants.

Writing the participants' stories and the stories of the victims gives testimony to the other side of the victims' official but untruthful documents, patient files, transportation lists, and death certificates with the fake date of death—all material constructed by the perpetrators. In this study I will give the family members and descendants a voice.

1.10 Definitions of Special Terms

Aesthetic analysis: I use the terms from Knill (*Principles and Practice of Expressive Arts Therapy: Towards a Therapeutic Aesthetics*) and Eberhart and Knill (*Lösungkunst, Lehrbuch der Kunst- und Ressourcenorientierten Arbeit*) and extended its meaning to the interview process. I used whatever came from the participants' description of surface elements, emotions, or remembered stories. During the aesthetic analysis, I encouraged the participants to look at their drawings at different levels, the surface of the artwork, the process of the art-making and the experience of it.

Euthanasia: In this study, Euthanasia refers to the brutal killings of unwanted people during the Nazi regime in Germany. The name is capitalized throughout the study to emphasize the weight of the crimes just as the word *Holocaust* is also capitalized. The term does not refer to the intentional ending of life to alleviate pain and suffering nor does it refer to assisted suicide.

Decentering: a term coined from Knill and Eberhart and Knill to be used in a therapeutic, counseling, or supervision session to shift focus from established ways of looking at an idea. I included the decentering in the interview based on my experience in the expressive arts.

Harvesting: as termed by Knill and Eberhart and Knill. While they refer to the problem stated in the beginning of the therapeutic, counseling or supervision session, I refer to and repeat the interview questions to the participants.

Interview: Used in this research in a dialogue fashion. Together with the interview participant, we viewed certain issues pertaining to the context of the study.

Meditation: I use the term *meditation* in the context of the aesthetic analysis during the decentering phase of the interview. The term is meant in the sense of thinking about something deeply and carefully, with a concentrated and relaxed mind.

Personal Vignettes: Included in this study are also personal writings, which I term *personal vignettes*. They are distinct from the main text of the study and marked with Futura typeface or set into a frame. Van Maanen calls these kinds of personal writings *confessional tales* (75).

1.11 Conceptual Foundations

In order to provide the conceptual context in which this work is placed, I shall describe the ideas, theories and personal experiences that have shaped both the concept and the following chapters of this study. I consider the Euthanasia crimes to be part of the Holocaust crimes perpetrated on Jewish people and other unwanted human beings, although under current German law, the victims are not regarded as victims of the Holocaust. Much has been published on the descendants of the perpetrators, and despite some descendants of perpetrators also regarding themselves as victims of and heirs to a terrible family history, I prefer to distance my inquiries from that particular perspective.

The stories of the participants are reflected in the interviews, which I conducted. The participants were handed or mailed a lay summary explaining the purpose of the study and the methods of how the interviews are conducted. I kept in contact through telephone conversations, visits, and mail contact with most of the participants throughout the study. All participants have given a written consent to have the interviews and their artwork published in this study.

The literature for this research examines the roots of the crimes, describes the methodological killings, and documents the effects that the crimes have on the following generations. With this background information, I examine how life is still worth living and how the descendants shaped their lives despite this burdensome heritage.

2.0 CONCEPTUAL CONTEXT

2.1 History of Crimes

> After the takeover of power in 1933, the Nazi regime changed the healthcare system in Germany. Developmentally disabled people and so-called *social misfits* were discriminated against: **410,000** people, [numbers of victims institutionalized before being Euthanized] were forcibly sterilized according to Lifton (25). Forced sterilizations are considered as predecessors to the Euthanasia murders (Lifton 22).
>
> From 1939 to 1945, approximately **275,000** (according to the results of the Nuremberg trial) as discussed on the Deathcamps organization on its website, adults and children became victims of Nazi Euthanasia crimes under the eugenic-based Euthanasia program. They died in gas chambers until the program was halted in 1941 yet continued through the so-called *wild Euthanasia* (Lifton 96-102) and was carried out through injections, overdosed medication, and starvation.
>
> According to the *Ausstellungsband "Euthanasie"-Verbrechen in Südwestdeutschland*, **70,000** people were murdered in the gas chambers of six psychiatric hospitals: Grafeneck, Hadamar, Bernburg, Brandenburg, Sonnenstein/Pirna, and Hartheim in Austria. This inclued from January to August 1941, **10,113** (George et al. 168) people were killed in the gas chambers of Hadamar. After the killings in the gas chamber was stopped, **4,411** (George et al 168) patients died between 1942 and 1945 through starvation and medication at the *Landesheilanstalt Hadamar*. To disguise the killings, a special agency was founded which issued death certificates. The families were supplied with a death certificate with a falsified cause of death. (George et al. 162).

The title of this study, *A LIFE Worthy of Life*, is a statement of affirmation which opposes the notion of "life unworthy of living" propounded by the legal scholar Karl Binding and the psychiatrist Alfred Hoche in their 1920 publication *Die Freigabe der Vernichtung lebensunwerten Lebens: Ihr Maß und ihre Form*, [*The Permission to Destroy Life Unworthy of Life: Its Extent and Form*]. Binding and Hoche sought to justify the killing of those who were "unheilbar blödsinnig, lebensunwert, geistig tote Menschen" (incurably stupid, unworthy of life, mentally dead people) (30). Their work provided the foundation for the principles of thought and action behind the murders and forced sterilizations carried out during the Nazi regime. In their publication, Binding and Hoche laid down criteria for those lives which, in their opinion, were worth living and those which were not—and could be ended (30, 49). They devised positivistic terminology for use in their writings of the *Die Freigabe der Vernichtung lebensunwerten Lebens: Ihr Maß und ihre Form* in order to justify and promote murders and forced sterilization. In their terminology, *murdering people* is phrased as *giving permission to murder*. In addition to giving permission, the murder is seen as something wanted by the people in order to release them of the burden of their own life. Binding/Hoche's work was published in 1920, just thirteen years before the Nazi regime came to power and nineteen years prior to Hitler's signing the authorization for the murders (Klee 458).

Dörner introduces the perspective from the history of industrial development and how it led to the marginalization of people who could not perform according to the standards of the industrial society. In Dörner's view, our present-day society evolved from a society based on family and philosophy, which embraced all kinds of people with different skills and mental capacity. The industrial revolution brought about a split in the system. Both the bourgeoisie and the blue-collar workers marginalized the mentally ill (21, 22).

Klee, in *"Euthanasie" im NS-Staat: Die "Vernichtung lebensunwerten Lebens"* [*Euthanasia in the Nazi State: The "Extermination of Life Not Worth Living"*] provides a chronology of the murders in relation to the development of World War II (458). He records the vicious aspects of the murders in detail based on documents from the archives of the Federal Republic of Germany and the former German Democratic Republic. He also describes the involvement of the Catholic and Protestant churches and charitable institutions and their staff. Klee describes how, even after the end of the war, the killings in the psychiatric hospitals continued (461).

Lifton, in *The Nazi Doctors, Medical Killing and the Psychology of Genocide*, offers a history and analysis of the role medical doctors played in Nazi genocide. He traces the medical killings and the workings of the concentration camps. His research includes interviews conducted with Nazi doctors, and he describes their view of the crimes they committed. "Mental hospitals became an important center for the developing 'Euthanasia' consciousness," he comments (48).

The former killing institution and now *Heil-und Pflegeanstalt* [sanatorium] in Hadamar was also the start of my research. My aunt, Anna Gerecht and Karoline V., Euthanasia victims portrayed in this study whose family members I interviewed, were both killed in this institution. Kneuker and Steglich in *Begegnungen mit der Euthanasie in Hadamar* [*Encounters with Euthanasia in Hadamar*] were the first to describe in detail the mass murders in Hadamar; and they also point out that even after the end of the war, the humiliation of the patients continued. They mention the case of a surviving patient who was used as a cheap laborer by the townspeople (101).

In their book, *Hadamar: Heilstätte, Tötungsanstalt, Therapiezentrum* [*Ha-damar: Sanitorium, Institution for Killing, Center for Therapy*], George et al. describe the Euthanasia crimes in the context of the original and present day usage of the buildings and facilities. Georg Lilienthal, one of the authors of this book, gives a detailed insight into the workings of the killing institution. He lists the sequence of events which comprised the ordered procedure starting with the grey buses, which collected the patients from the different psychiatric hospitals and brought them to a specially built, almost windowless garage shielded from the view of passers-by. From here people were herded through a covered passageway to be registered, photographed, and medically examined. Naked and humiliated, they were pushed down the stairs to their death in the gas chambers (159).

The personal fate of patients of the *Heil- und Pflegeanstalt Emmendingen* is described by Richter in his publication *Die Fahrt ins Graue(n)* [*Journey into Horror(s)*]. Richter also encouraged me to contact a co-author of his publication and descendant of a Euthanasia victim. The *Heil-und Pflegeanstalt Emmendingen* is also the institution were one of the victims portrait in this study died.

Meckel, in her publication *Den Opfern ihre Namen zurückgeben* [*To Give the Victims Their Names Back*], documents the *Stolpersteineprojekt*, the small memorials which commemorate the victims of the Euthanasia and Holocaust crimes on small brass plaques embedded in the sidewalks of the streets and in front of the houses where the victims lived before being deported. Her book lists the plaques and names of the victims as well as the biographical data.

> The memorials inscribed with the names of the victims touched me very deeply. The small plaques seem to bridge time and space. They are situated in front of the homes were people lived their daily lives. I imagine the women, men and children being led out and taken away to their death in the concentration camps. They lived an ordinary life, until one day their lives are deemed not worth living.

2.1.1 Literature on the Descendants of the Euthanasia and Holocaust Victims

Delius and Fleßner are among the few scholars who have carried out research on the descendants of Euthanasia victims and the impact the crimes have had on their lives. Delius described in a case study how one family member of a Euthanasia victim feared that he had a hereditary disease. This dread led to the fear of getting married because of the possibility of having disabled children. The taboo on speaking about a disabled family member is particularly strong: There is the fear of being identified with the carrier of "bad blood." The fear associated with a decades-long taboo and the presence of a family secret presents a significant burden on the family members (33, 64). Delius also conducted observations of his own intrapsychic processing of the Euthanasia murders (31).

Fleßner adds to Delius' observations that there is not only a taboo in the families with regard to the Euthanasia victim but also a taboo on speaking of the Nazi past openly. The current effort to repeal the law preventing hereditary diseases and to compensate victims for forced sterilization puts the issue in the spotlight of the public, an opportunity to break the manifold taboo (163).

Bar-On makes a major contribution to the literature of the Holocaust and to the literature of the descendents of victims and perpetrators. He talks about how the state of victimhood has been passed on to the next generation through the building of walls of silence between the members of the different generations (*Die Last des Schweigens* 33). Bar-On explains that parents cannot protect the children from their oppressive memories, even if guilt prevents them from talking. The barely hinted-at stories persist, passing from one generation to another more often than stories, which are told and discussed. In his introduction, Bar-On in *Hoffnung bis zu den Enkeln des Holocausts* reflects on the possibility of stopping the cycle of victimhood. He uses the metaphor of a tree to express how the vision of a life worth living is possible by grafting the healthy, vital parts of the self onto new and healthy roots. That means to recognize and work through the feelings of alienation (II). How can the descendants of the Euthanasia victims live with the fear of heredity disease, the shame of having a disabled relative with no possibility to grieve for the murdered relative, and to accept the helplessness of the contemporary family members and still live a meaningful life?

2.1.2 Literature on Intrapsychic Effects of the Nazi Regime

Four publications cited in this study refer to the intrapsychic effects of the Nazi regime: The titles of the following publications refer to the intrapsychic effects: Müller-Hohagen's *History in Us*, Gruen's *The Stranger in Us*, and Dörner in *Tödliches Mitleid* speaks about "the Nazi in us" (13).

Müller-Hohagen describes the psychic impact on the descendants of Nazi perpetrators and bystanders. He talks of their loyalty to their parents (45). I would suggest that this loyalty could be extended to the family secret: Disclosing the family secret would mean being disloyal to the family, but it is an opportunity for the descendants to overcome the restrictions set by the family.

Müller-Hohagen states that the trauma of the Holocaust is very much a reality for the children of Holocaust victims, despite the parents' not revealing their experiences. In families where the parents are Holocaust survivors, the extremely traumatic background of the parents often cannot be told to the children; yet the children are very aware of the trauma of the Holocaust in the family (22). The same is valid for the descendants of the Euthanasia victims as this study will show.

Helen Epstein, an American journalist and daughter of Holocaust survivors, could not talk to her parents, so she went on a search to find people like herself who were living "under the spell of a story they had not experienced". She did not experience the Holocaust herself, but her life experience was shaped by her parents' fate as Holocaust survivors. Epstein was hoping to reach that part of her which had eluded her most persistently (qtd. in Müller-Hohagen 23).

The feeling Epstein refers to, of being "under the spell of" a phenomenon, was also experienced very intensely by a participant of this study: that of being "under the spell of" her grandmother. In my own family, my brother Karl, whom I interviewed for this study, and I myself, also felt the shadow of our aunt's murder, even though it was not discussed. There were no feelings of sadness or anger expressed in my family during my childhood.

Gruen argues that feelings of emotional coldness, grief, hopelessness, helplessness, or powerlessness while experiencing higher levels of stress emerge through not being in control of one's life (10). These feelings are also present in family members of Euthanasia victims. In his study, families who care for each other have a more satisfying life. In fact, his conclusion is that people live longer not only by not striving for money and possessions but also by belonging to the community and also through allowing pain to be present and to be experienced. They can live a life worthy of living (212). Gruen mentions the Brazilian pedagogue Paulo Freire in his attempt to show how hopefulness and poetry writing can better an individual's situation and help him/her find satisfaction and overcome barriers, even in a very restricted environment (202).

I am drawn to read Alexander and Margarete Mitscherlich. They address the German society of perpetrators and this contention in the foreword to their book, "That in German society, the confrontation with the repressed contents of the consciousness and unconscious of the Nazi regime is not yet completed" (II). Like the perpetrators, the descendants of

> WATER'S EDGE
> Standing by the lake shore,
> remembering the ocean.
> Looking back and grieve:
> rebuilding a new life.
>   Sarva Posey

Euthanasia victims are blocked in their ability to think about the implications on their lives. The Mitscherlichs propose that when people no longer dare to ask or even imagine asking a question, they are coming up against a taboo. A taboo functions as an effective regulator of people's behavior, like a higher authority, and does not tolerate opposition (111).

Dörner also acknowledges that today, groups of people with a disability can speak for themselves and are more integrated into mainstream society. It had become quite usual for representatives of the victims of forced sterilization, the Sinti and Roma people, Euthanasia victims, homosexuals, and social outcasts to speak for themselves for the first time in history (85). The participants in this study are speaking for the descendants of the Euthanasia victims.

Naomia, a survivor of the Lodz Ghetto, touches on the issue that violence can produce more violence: "Hitler still can fulfill his goal of eradicating the Jewish people, if we as Jewish people internalize the hate, distrust, the pain and the whole inhumanity to which we have been exposed for many years. Before the Holocaust we had the ability to trust and love" (qtd. in Bar-On 55). The same is valid for the descendants of the Euthanasia victims: Mistrust and self-hate can make one's life very difficult. On the other hand, Bar-On also explores the possibilities of deriving meaning from the Holocaust crimes. According to Bar-On, the search for hope has to do with the recognition of truth (*Die Last des Schweigens* 65).

2.1.3 Literature on Shame

Tiedemann researches the phenomenon of shame and the displacement of shame expressed in resentment while Perner speaks of the power of "taboo" in the family. Tiedemann examines the function of shame and how shame and guilt are interconnected. He explains shame in relationship to the "quality of the self."

Tiedemann also writes about shame and disgrace and sees a connection between shame and guilt distinguishing between the sufferings caused by each. He sees the suffering caused by shame as being more existential than suffering due to feelings of guilt. Shame acts to cause the personality to disintegrate through disgrace. A shamed person can feel small and despicable and without dignity. The damage caused by shame is irreparable (17, 18). The taboo to speak about secrets can contribute to shame.

> I experienced the ambivalent feeling of "outing" myself as a researcher. I was afraid of becoming taboo to my family by crossing the threshold, wanting to gain knowledge.
> Sarva Posey

Perner describes how the family structure keeps the taboo of the family secret in place. A way to cope with the taboo in the family is to retreat into an inner emigration (8).

Another aspect of the taboo in the family is as Perner describes: The person who concerns him/herself with the taboo in the family may become taboo him/herself. Perner continues that only somebody who sticks to the rules can stay in the community (171). Breaking the taboo in the family breaks the unwritten rules of not talking about the murdered Euthanasia victim.

2.1.4 Literature on the Descendants of the Perpetrators

Gruen, Müller-Hohagen, and Mitscherlich address the intrapsychic effects of the Nazi regime on the descendants of the victims as well as on the descendants of the perpetrators and bystanders to the crimes. As some of the participants of this study are also descendants of perpetrators and bystanders (e.g. family members who were part of the army), it is sometimes hard to distinguish between the impact of being a descendant of a perpetrator or bystander and that of being the descendant of a victim. Perpetrators and bystanders both consider themselves to be victims of the circumstances. Looking back at my own family history, my father considered himself more as a victim of the circumstances of World War II started by the Nazi regime than as the brother of a victim of Euthanasia crimes carried out by the same people.

Gruen writes that the perpetrators actually felt that they were victims and that the sense of being a victim is transferred from one generation to the next. He theorizes that people murder because they do not have their own story; they are the ones actually dead.

The hatred of strangers or in this study hatred of disabled people is perhaps a result of self-hatred (58). As a researcher and descendant, I try to understand why these crimes were committed.

Bar-On (*Die Last des Schweigens*), Delius (*Nationalsozialistische Gewaltmassnahmen gegen psychisch Kranke, Die Psychisch Kranken Opfer des Nationalsozialismus und ihre Familien*), and in particular Dörner include themselves in their potential as perpetrators. Dörner calls this experience, "Walking in the shoes of the perpetrator." For a long time, Dörner believed that his sense of being a potential Nazi too was his own personal perception. His views allowing the possibility, however, as providing a chance to acknowledge this tendency without submitting to it (9).

2.2 Personal Context

My own biographical data, spiritual literature, the issue of different and diverse languages, and my reflections on people with disability have shaped my subjective self as it pertains to this study. With this in mind, I acknowledge that personal issues and perspectives shift constantly and are created and recreated throughout the research process.

As a young person, reading spiritual literature and practicing meditation was a way of coping with the contradictory messages I was receiving from society in terms of values and principles, and providing help in navigating through my life and serving as a form of self-care. Literature from Eastern religious and spiritual traditions has had a strong impact on my thinking. Pema Chödrön, a Buddhist teacher, speaks from the Buddhist point of view about loss and tragedy and the acceptance of these as life experience by being present (6-11). During the last few years I have practiced guided meditation, inducing physical relaxation with a *body scan meditation* (103-112) and *cultivating mindfulness* (53) as described by Williams et al. Jack Kornfield has guided my understanding of Buddhist psychology and my understanding of the notion of *loving kindness* (2). I used this meditation technique to lean against my own negative mind and the rage and anger coming up during the time of this research.

The wish to strengthen my ability to reflect on my own research process led me to explore once again the practice of contemplative meditation appropriate to my age and station in life. Another way to reflect is employing the visual arts and using the senses in expressing myself. Osho, whose meditations are available on the Osho website, uses Western psychology and Eastern meditation techniques to find a way through inner turmoil to be present and to experience presence with all the senses.

The inner attitude I have developed gives meaning to my life and carries me through life and this research process. Having been on a spiritual journey since my early adulthood, I can look at events in my life and at my own victimhood in a conscious and accepting way, finding some closure to continue my journey. There is a tendency in me to reject the role of being a victim as I consider it a weakness. At times, a daily practice of meditation helps me to negotiate the difficulties, which arise through this process of research into my own family trauma, and to be present in relationship with the participants of this study.

As an artist, I see and relate to the world through a visual lens which is also alive and moving. I can also relate to the architects Peter Zumthor's way of perceiving a given project as a sensory image. Zumthor writes, "When I work on a design I allow myself to be guided by images and moods that I remember and can relate to the kind of architecture I am looking for" (25). As an architect, I rely on my sensory awareness. I imagine walking through the buildings as I design the structure, always looking for interesting perspectives and surprises.

2.2.1 Bias and Subjectivity

On and off throughout my life, I have thought about my Aunt Anna, a Euthanasia victim who was killed in the gas chambers of Hadamar. In fact, growing up in the sixties, I was aware of the Nazi atrocities and could not understand how my father could go to war for the same regime that killed his sister. Wolcott reminds us that our preconceived notions of our working lives, our personalities, and our situations are the beginnings of our research considerations (408).

My own and my family's history make me who I am as a person. I am biased because of my biography, the events that shaped my life, my work in different professions, travel, and moves to different countries. I have transplanted myself many times starting at the age of 18, exploring alternative and seemingly opposite life styles by both living in alternative communities and being a career woman, having a traditional married life and being divorced, being an architect, artist, massage therapist, and expressive arts therapist. I sense with Glesne that "Some hints of subjectivities might be called into play during your research, can be foreshadowed by reflecting on how your research is autobiographical" (106).

I grew up with the unspoken and a taboo in the family. Breaking the taboo by researching into the life of my Aunt Anna, I also forgo my role of the victim. Researching the life of Anna and her victimhood, I explore my own life and my role as a victim. I feel a deep vulnerability through the fact that a member of my close family was murdered as a patient in a psychiatric hospital.

2.2.2 Language, Language Barriers and Voices

The issues which surround language are ever present in this study. Although I am a German native speaker, I have chosen to write this study in the English language making translation an integral part of my reading, writing, and thinking. Reading the literature, I move between the German language and the English language with ease and understanding. I think and write in both languages. Nevertheless, finding a crossover between the two languages is challenging, and my intuitive approach to translate from one language to the other is difficult to describe. Language usage and the meaning of words are embedded in the German or English language world experience. Certain words are loaded with more emotional content in one language. These words are often connected with difficult feelings. Sometimes I cannot express a feeling in German, and I use the English language to verbalize it.

In this study, to code the theme of shame, I had to translate parts of the interviews into the English language. I used the English language to circumvent the difficulties and the intrapsychic effect of shame I had in recognizing shame as an emotion in the German language transcript. At times I can express the meaning of an emotion more freely in the English language due to the extended therapy I underwent in the medium of the English language.

Most of the time now, I speak in my native tongue, meaning I speak with the inflections in my voice and language, which are indigenous to my hometown. When I listen to the voices of the participants in this study on the recorder, I feel reassured by hearing the authenticity of their spoken word. Sadly, I cannot translate the inflections in their voices into the English language.

Whatever the language, it is not only the choice of words but also the tone of voice which indicates intended and sometimes unintended meaning. The voice can betray the emotions underlying what is being said.

In this study, in order to expand my understanding of what has been said, I have listened carefully to the voice of the participant: The voice is a bridge to the written word. I hear the participants and my voice on the recorder and can feel our connection. Listening to the voice helps me to write in a lively way.

Sometimes in my writings for this study, I spontaneously change the language, choosing to write the field log and diary in English or in German according to my mood or the issue at hand. However, I acknowledge my handicap in both languages as a dyslexic; spelling and grammar, even in my native language, were never my forte. I am, however, a keen and curious observer, which is a prerequisite for telling a good story.

I have a tendency to look at the downside of being bilingual. This habit of focusing on the limitation can be a burden. Yet in pointing out this limitation, I also see an opportunity. I am drawn to challenges as a means of gaining self-knowledge about both my abilities and my limitations.

As language and the limitations of language are important issues in this research, so is issue of disability. I discuss my personal experience with disabled and differently-abled people in the next section.

2.2.3 Meetings with Differently-abled People

> During an expressive arts day workshop at the Appalachian State University, I met Kate, a severely disabled and differently-abled woman. We spent the day making nametags and hats together. At the end of the workshop, we danced to an upbeat piece of music. After a while, I picked up her movements and synchronized my steps with her. That was a most difficult but also satisfying experience on this day. I remember our dance because I made an effort to fall into step with Kate.

As a child I got a different message from the one I learned from Kate about disabled people. I remember that my mother, a trained nurse, used their being different as a threat to us children: "If you do not behave, you will end up in Ursberg," she would say. Ursberg is a large psychiatric hospital near the village where my mother grew up. Talk about disability was not part of our family life, even though my father and his sister had disabilities. As family members, we were considerate towards my father's disability. He was severely wounded as a soldier in the World War II and had to have a leg amputated. His sister's disability was not talked about. Mental illness was taboo in my family.

My father used to complain that some people felt that working in a plant nursery was for the disabled. He felt humiliated and mortified when teachers from special education schools came and asked for students to be placed as workers in the nursery. He worked very hard, harder than able-bodied people, so that people would not recognize his own disability.

In contrast to my own family, Richards has another view of differently-abled people as she called her housemates at a community in which she lived. In her DVD, she sees the disabled people she worked together with as possessing a kind of genius, differently-abled in their own world and in the world of art-making (2003). Richards poses a similar question to the one I asked myself before falling into step with Kate: how relate to each other coming from such different world experience.

In my work as an expressive art therapist, in the therapeutic session, I focus on the abilities and resources of the clients. Some of the clients' physical and cognitive abilities are limited. Sometimes the patients can create beautiful works alone; sometimes I assist the client in the execution of an artwork. As I also learn from my clients, it is a give and take situation.

It is different when I meet people with disability in an everyday setting. I am focused on my own business of daily chores and maybe feel hurried. I feel distanced; as I would from any other stranger I meet on the street, yet somehow I am drawn to the unusual behavior or appearance of the people with disability.

> On Thursday, I went to the supermarket after work. In the big parking lot outside, a van pulled in. A group of people excitedly stepped out of the van. In the way they moved with their bodies, from the expressions on their faces, and from the way they wore their clothes, I perceived them to be mentally and physically disabled people. A man and a woman were chaperoning them, almost herding them, touching them reassuringly. I went inside the store; it was midday and the store was almost empty. After a while a disabled man was shouting across the aisles. That was just the way he communicated, expressing his excitement. Shoppers turned their heads. A disabled man chatted with the cashier and asked her name. He brought such humanity into this sterile environment where customers are normally just seen as a means of gaining money.

People with disability, together with their caregivers, live in a different world. On this occasion, I kept a physical distance, yet my eyes and ears were drawn to them.

2.3 Summary

The descendants of Euthanasia victims are a population which is not widely researched, even though the impact of these crimes reverberate today and will continue into future generations. There seems to be a taboo around the issue of having had a disabled family member and a notion that the so-called "bad blood" in the family is hereditary: perhaps a disease that can be inherited from the Euthanasia victim. Shame connected with disability is particularly present with the descendants of Euthanasia victims.

Making disclosures and talking about the disabled family member with a stranger and a researcher is a hurdle for many descendants. That there has been a family member who was a Euthanasia victim is often a family secret. Talking about issues, which were secret for a long time, can be connected with intensive feelings of shame as Tiedemann (21) describes. Being myself a descendant of a Euthanasia victim and working with disabled patients may have helped me to gain the trust of the participants in this study so that they were able to open up and tell their stories, even to a stranger.

3.0 METHODOLOGICAL FRAMEWORK AND RESEARCH DESIGN

> "It will be obvious that radical constructivism itself must not be interpreted as a picture or description of any absolute reality but as a possible model of knowing and the acquisition of knowledge in cognitive organisms that are capable of constructing for themselves, on the basis of their own experience, a more or less reliable world" (von Glasersfeld 18).

The assembly of methods used for this research is grouped under the broad headings of qualitative inquiry, decentering, and arts-based research with the theoretical orientation of constructivism and phenomenological research. In the research design section, I explain how the data is collected and how the findings of the study are constructed. The research design overlaps with the conceptual context, as described in the previous chapter.

Not only concept and methodology are interwoven, but also questions of research methods are seen as aspects of the whole. To rephrase Kriz, the *Welt- und Menschenbild* [*Concept of the World and Humanity*], the conceptual context, questions and hypotheses, the methodology and the method belong to the whole (71). Qualitative, ethnographic and autoethnographic, and phenomenological research literature as well as post-qualitative and arts-based literatures are the nuts and bolts that join the framework of this study together.

The St. Pierre post-qualitative methods of decentering are applied in this study. St. Pierre uses decentering as a general approach to investigation and specifically as a way of decentering the voice from the narrative (319) and going beyond conventional qualitative research.

I am also using the term *decentering* as used in the expressive arts work of Eberhart and Knill (101). I conceptualized the interview process and its design in accordance with their expressive arts approach of a therapeutic session, except in the harvesting part of the decentering. The expressive arts capture the way we express ourselves in this study, which goes beyond qualitative research. Levine describes going beyond qualitative research as, "The task of our thinking is to capture the aliveness of our being, to follow it and help express itself in words " (154).

The core research method is a collective case study (Stake 22) where participants, the descendants of Euthanasia victims, tell their stories through interviews and art-making. Poetry is used in the cross-case analysis (Stake 39) and as a method of reflection. As Leavy states, "Poems, surrounded by space and heightened by silence, break through the noise to present an essence … poems push feelings to the forefront capturing heightened moments of social reality as if under a magnifying glass" (63). The interlocking components of excerpts from interviews as well as reflections, essays, poetry, and visual arts support the emerging themes of the study. Poems also reflect my personal feelings in regards to the issues, and they underline the subjective nature of this study.

Woven into the design of the methodological structure are the biases and subjectivity of my dual roles as researcher and participant. Like Jill in Glesne's *Becoming Qualitative Researchers: An Introduction*, I felt that I had found a "research home" when I learned that qualitative research existed. The "frame of these research methods and methodology" has enabled me to write the stories of the descendants of Euthanasia victims; and with them, I have written "my own story" (8).

3.1 Methodology

The methodology of this study is qualitative, ethnographic, autoethnographic, post-qualitative and arts-based research drawn from the research literature. Qualitative research describes the method of data collection and analysis. Ethnographic and autoethnographic research literature depicts the way to tell the participants and my own story. Post-qualitative and arts-based literature describes decentering the voice with the arts.

3.1.1 Qualitative Research

Glesne and Creswell provide a basic understanding of qualitative research, the use of language and its application, and the methods of data collection and analysis. Whereas Glesne focuses more on subjective, personal investigation, Creswell has developed a theory of a spiral approach to the data analysis. My procedure for documenting leans on Glesne's constructivist paradigm of qualitative inquiry and tries to mirror the reality of an ever-changing world. (5). The coding system I developed was based on Creswell's approach to the collection and analysis of data and the writing of reports as being concurrent and not proceeding in isolation (150). Creswell explains "Looking over our field notes, interview data, physical trace evidence, and audio and visual images, we disregarded predetermined questions so we could hear what interviewees said. We reflected on the larger thoughts presented in the data and formed initial categories" (151). I started with writing essays, finding categories, and through analysis identified the themes which were supported across the participants' stories, interview questions, and in the literature.

> "These characteristics are that the research takes place in the natural setting, employs multiple methods of data collection, is emergent rather than prefigured, is based on the interpretations of the researcher, is viewed holistically,

is reflective, uses both inductive and deductive reasoning processes, and employs a strategy of inquiry" (Creswell 205).

Other writers acknowledge agreement with the above concepts (Patton, 2002; Denzin and Lincoln, 2003; Gay and Airasian, 2003; Yow, 2004).

3.1.2 Autoethnography and Ethnography

Glesne's subjective approach continues in her engagement with the issue of autoethnography: "As the writer of the study, autoethnography begins with the self, the personal biography and is part of the sociocultural context" (181). Extending Glesne's discussion, Ellis points out ways to position the autoethnographic self in relation to the research: not just to tell one's own story but also to assist others in telling theirs (72). Writing my autoethnographical narrative allowed me to bring my own family trauma closer to the people I interviewed. Ellis refers to autoethnographical narrative as a form of reading, writing, storytelling, and art-making that connects the personal to the cultural, social and political (121). Sociologist and postmodern ethnographer Linden writes about the Holocaust from an autoethnographic point of view. Her work highlights the relationship of the researcher to the participant both as observer and peer. She states, "I can ask no less of myself than I ask of my ethnographic subjects. I must be prepared to be at least as vulnerable and honest as I ask them to be. I must be willing to stand beside them, not to speak *for* them but to speak for myself and *with* them" (ix). This attitude is how I aspire to conduct myself as a researcher and participant in this study. Van Maanen states that we cannot represent others in any other terms but our own. In his view, culture is something we construct and is method and methodology (12). In this study, the participants are introduced with my impression of their home environment and how I perceive their *outer appearance*. To rephrase Van Maanen: My attempt is to evoke an open, participatory sense in the viewer and maybe startle the viewer out of a complacent and detached view to research (101).

3.1.3 Post-qualitative: Decentering and Arts-Based Research

St. Pierre refers to post-qualitative inquiry as "decentering the voice." According to her, decentering the voice refers to a method of qualitative inquiry distinct from phonocentrism. This method enables an inquiry that may no longer be recognized as "qualitative" (319) in the conventional sense of the term. In my study, I accept the authorial stance that St. Pierre suggests: Post-modern researchers should remain self-speculative about voice and also see decentering the voice as opening up the research to visual art-making and poetry. Knill in *Principle and Practice of Expressive Arts Therapy* uses decentering to increase the range of play, facilitating the artistic experience. In addition, he talks about the ethnographic aspects of therapy in rites of passage and rites of restoration as a way to "re-search" (77, 79). Knill states, "In the imaginary space that is emerging, things are in their surprising unpredictable unexpectedness, but they still possess a logic and are describable … Therefore change agents apply methods bridging the two experiences in order to find inroads for change and clarification" (81). In this study, as the researcher I take the position of the change agent.

While St. Pierre also sees poetry as decentering from the narrative, and Knill uses poetry in the decentering phase of the session; Leavy employs poetry as a method of arts-based research. Leavy proposes, "Poetry as a research strategy challenges the fact-fiction dichotomy and offers a form for the evocative presentation of data" (63). In this study, I use poetry to show the participants' commonalities and diversities as part of the collective case study.

Another aspect of post-qualitative research is the researcher-participant relationship. My relationship to the participants has shaped this study throughout the research and interview process. St. Pierre emphasizes, "One aspect of post-qualitative research involves the researcher being present in relationship with the participants" (326). Being present is both a philosophical concept and a post-qualitative research method. This experience is a metaphysical construct that "has always designated the relationship with a presence" (Derrida qtd.in. St. Pierre 326). Being present in listening to the narrative of the participant was vital to this study and the open-ended nature of the questions. Williams, Mark, et al. point out that presence is also expressed as mindfulness and awareness in the Eastern meditative traditions (54 passim). As a researcher and as a person, I subscribe wholeheartedly to the need to be present in the verbal communication and the art-making with participant. The study is designed to reflect our meeting as it occurred.

3.2 Research Design

This arts-based collective case study portrays six participants as they describe their common experience of being descendents of Euthanasia victims. In this section, I describe how I met the participants, the time and place for the interview, and how I prepared for the art-making part. The research design section outlines how I logged the research experience and the interview process including the arts-based strategies and how the data was produced by these strategies. The research design section also *includes my perception of the research process as both researcher and participant.*

3.2.1 Qualitative Narrative Inquiry

This study is an inquiry into the participants' daily lives: what makes life worthy of living, their family relationships, and the possible implications of having a Euthanasia victim in the family. Glesne (4) and von Glasersfeld (9) define qualitative research as "ways of knowing" in which the knowing comes from lived experience rather than from measurable facts. This model of inquiry provides the freedom to interact with the participants through open-ended questions during the interview.

In this study, I ask the participants to look at aspects of their lives which offer gratification and also aspects which are difficult for them before inquiring about their knowing of the Euthanasia victim. Being a descendant of a Euthanasia victim is just one aspect of the participant's life. What the participants said in conversations on the phone and in e-mail correspondence changed over the years, reflecting the changes in the participants' lives. To rephrase von Glasersfeld, the study is structured to reflect how the participants experience their world and how I perceive the spoken word of the participants (9).

3.2.2 Arts-Based Collective Case Study

The fundamental design of the study grows out of arts-based research based on qualitative inquiry described in the previous section. While asking multifold questions during the interview, I paint a picture in my mind about the issues at hand, asking the participant for his or her responses and interpretations. Visual arts, essays, and poetry are modalities that I used in this study.

In this multicase study (Stake vi), I used questions to guide the insight into the lives of the participants. My inquiry was about the participants' lives in general, what gives them pleasure, what is difficult for them, and what is the unspoken in the families.

This arts-based collective case study reports on the quality of life and family relationships of the participant. Attention in the study is paid to the individual participant and the commonality of being a descendant. The emerging themes shed light on the issue of being a descendant in the context of lived experience.

Meeting the Participants

I enjoy meeting people. I enrich my thinking by being in relationship. I learn about the world and myself. I live and reflect on what it means to be a descendant and family member of a Euthanasia victim. Interviewing the participants makes me feel part of a family.

With the questions in mind posed in the previous section, I began to seek out potential participants. I met these people at gatherings of a support association and through researchers in the field of Nazi Euthanasia crimes and the Holocaust.

Two participants are members of my own family. The oldest person I interviewed was Günter Schreiber. Marlis Meckel introduced me to Günter Schreiber, a second-generation family member.

I met Erika and Beate Schneider (pseudonyms), mother and daughter, second and third generation descendents, at a gathering commemorating a memorial site and celebrating the anniversary of the Förderverein [*support association*]. Erika Schneider invited me, a stranger, to join in a discussion at her table. After a while, I introduced myself and explained my wish to carry out this study, distributing the lay summary.

Gardy Ruder is a third-generation family member of a Euthanasia victim. I was familiar with her name from a newspaper article she had published about the life of her grandmother. Dr. Gabriel Richter, author and a leading physician at the psychiatric hospital in Emmendingen, suggested that I approach Gardy Ruder.

My brother Karl Gerecht and Christine Garden (pseudonym), a family member, agreed to be interviewed for this study in support of my inquiry into our family history. Several other family members contributed their recollections to this study.

One participant decided not to continue with the study after some month. Mrs. Weber (pseudonym) decided to discontinue her participation in the research. There was a chasm we could not overcome. Events in her life may have contributed to her decision, and possibly also she experienced her participation in the study as a burden.

I will present the writings of this study to the participants and ask for their consent again. As Glesne writes: "It is understood that the informed consent process is dynamic and continuous … by the way of dialog and negotiation … it is the quality of the consent not the format that is relevant" (17).

Preparing an Arts-Based Inquiry

When I arranged with the participants where and when to conduct the interview, I left the choice of venue to them. They choose to be in their own homes where I quickly had to find my bearings and to familiarize myself with the surroundings. I made sure there was a separate space to conduct the interview and the art-making part. Time was another factor to consider in designing the sequence of the interview. As Knill argues, "The strict temporal and spatial structures, for instance, found in scheduling, contracts, room arrangements, substances, language … can be considered ritualistic from a phenomenological perspective" (111). Time and space are part of the structure and ritual of a therapeutic session.

In the context of this study, I collected accounts of specific qualities in the lives of the participants as well as qualities of being a descendant of a Euthanasia victim. I tried to show as many facets as possible of the participants' personalities and also to come close to the issue of family secrets and the experience of being a descendant of a Euthanasia victim. Art-making was embedded in the interview with the method of decentering followed by the aesthetic analysis. Harvesting concluded the interview.

The arts-based inquiry phase of the interview was designed to take 20 minutes. This restricted time frame removes the pressure to create something special and allows the person to stay with sketchy images. However, most of the participants took about 30 minutes to conclude the artwork.

Prior to starting the art-making, I introduced the participants to the materials I provided. These materials consisted of heavyweight, off-white drawing paper, 29 x 42 centimeters, and a large box of good quality pastel crayons and charcoal pencils. The choice of materials was tailored to the limited time frame, ease of use, and the location unknown to me. To give a sense of choice and control, participants could choose to reduce the paper size or use more than one sheet of paper. The pastel crayons provided were usually easy to use and did not require special skills. The brilliance of the colors made an immediate impression that motivated the participants to explore colors and shapes on the paper. I did a short demonstration to illustrate the use of the crayons; however, drawing with these small crayons was not easy for everybody. There was a possibility for using fingers and smudging the applied colors, which underlined the playful aspect of the art-making activity. Some of the participants did not use their fingers. One participant used some of his own charcoal pencils. Before starting the drawings, I asked the participants to take a minute to close their eyes, feel their feet on the floor, listen to the sounds and see if there were any images that wanted to be expressed.

I suggest that being present in the body can be helpful to be present for the task ahead. I asked the participants to look at the colors, choose one that appealed to them, and to start with a hand movement. While I explained this process, I moved my own hand.

> I look intensely
> at the box of crayons,
> imagining some rich
> Chocolate truffles.
> I am eager to taste with my eyes,
> the brilliant and muted
> shades of the colors.
> Sarva Posey

Logging the Research Experience

To negotiate the terrain and the environment of each participant's life and my own learning, I kept a field log and diary from the beginning of the research. The field log recorded the meetings, emails, and telephone conversations with the participants, family members, researchers in the field, and institutions and government agencies. I recorded my reflections on the literature relating to the concept and methodology of this study. The field log and the diary also included essays and poetry.

Writing the diary is a form of self-care where I unloaded personal struggles and triumphs. The diary recounts the emotional upheaval I experienced as a researcher and participant and reflects personal changes throughout the research process. The emotional engagement and the distance or closeness I felt towards the respective participants was recorded in personal reflections. Field log and diary complement the interview transcriptions and art works discussed in the next section.

Interviews and Arts-Based Strategies

When I decided to conduct interviews with the descendants of the Euthanasia victims, I relied on my experience as an expressive arts therapist. Using decentering with art-making helped deepen the issues for the participants. The initial questions I asked in the interview helped the participants to muster their own resources and coping strategies before approaching the issue of the murdered relative. I did not want the issue of Euthanasia to dominate the interview from the start, but first I needed to get a sense of how the participants experienced life.

3.3 Interview

The interviews were conducted in German, as all participants are native Ger-man-speakers. The quotations from the interviews may lose some of their original flavor as the special nuances of a particular German dialect are difficult to convey in translation. The interviews were sequenced through three sections. In the first section, I asked six questions about the quality of the participants' present lives, their current family relationships, and their knowledge of and response to the life and death of the Euthanasia victim. During the second section of the interview, we engaged in decentering through art-making and an aesthetic analysis of the art product and the process of art-making. In the third part of the interview, the harvesting, I repeated the questions from the beginning of the interview. The participant had the opportunity to elaborate and report on any changes, which had occurred in, and after the decentering phase of the interview.

To develop the interview questions, I turned to the topic of being a descendant of a Euthanasia victim and asked myself the questions, paraphrasing Glesne (69): I wanted the participants to be able to speak about their feelings towards the family member who was not only disabled but also a victim of Euthanasia and the implications of this fact for their own lives. I adopted a strategy based on my experience as an expressive arts therapist. I assumed from my work with traumatized patients that reminding people of their own resources could help them to cope with difficult questions that arise. If I want to understand about the participants' lives and the unspoken in the families, which questions do I have to ask? With the first question I asked the participants about their resources and coping strategies:

> 1st What do you do to relax or for recreation after a workday, and what helps you to cope with your daily life?

In the second three-fold challenging question, I asked the participant to de-scribe, reflect on, and respond to what they like and dislike about themselves and talk of a specific difficult situation they had experienced. This situation could be taken from their professional or private life:

> 2nd What is it about yourself that pleases you, and what causes displeasure? When somebody treats you unjustly, how do you respond? Can you describe a situation in which you were treated unjustly?

Questions three to six addressed the family life of the participants and the knowledge of the Euthanasia victim. The participants were asked to think of a situation, which had occurred at some time during a family gathering. Engaging in active, prompted recollection in the interview helped them to recall past events such as the situation in which they first gained knowledge about the victim. A shared experience could have been that at family gatherings.

> 3rd Could you please describe a family party, birthday or Christmas holiday in your family of origin? Please describe your family relationships.

I designed questions four to six more specifically to explore the participants' feelings regarding the family secret and the family member who was a Euthanasia victim. I wanted to address the participants' knowledge of the existence of this person and their emotional responses to him or her:

> 4th How do you know of and cope with events in the family which are not spoken of? Would you give me an example please?

5th When and where did you hear for the first time that your father, grandmother, aunt/great-aunt was killed at (name of the killing institution)?

6th How do you talk in your family about your father, grandmother, aunt/great-aunt, (the Euthanasia victim) and what are your feelings when the issue comes up?

After the participants had answered the initial questions, we took a short break and moved to the atelier where we continued with the decentering phase of the interview.

3.3.1 Decentering

I have adapted the method of decentering in expressive arts therapy as described by both Knill and Knill and Eberhart for use as a research strategy. Decentering is a method used in expressive arts therapy counseling and supervision to gain distance from the issues discussed in a session. Knill describes decentering as follows: "By decentering we name the move away from the narrow logic of thinking and acting that marks the helplessness around the 'dead-end' situation in question. This is a move into the opening of surprising unpredictable unexpectedness, the experience within the logic of imagination" (83). In the interview, I offered a distance to the interview questions by encouraging the participants to draw whatever came to their minds whether it was connected with the context of the interview.

Incorporating art-making as decentering in the interview can change the quality of the story. Atkins states that the expressive arts give an additional dimension and depth to the work with the arts. She points out that art-making gives access to emotions and insights, which are not easily accessed by verbal communication (7). In this study, the imagination finds expression by means of color and crayons, using the hands, and the movement of the hands.

3.3.2 Aesthetic Preliminary Analysis

After the decentering process with art-making, we proceeded with the aesthetic analysis. I moved over from the interview space where I wrote down some notes while the participants did their drawing. I pulled up a chair and sat next to the participant in the atelier, and we shared our impressions of the drawing and the participant's experience of the process.

The aesthetic analysis of the artwork is the closest I can come to being able to understand the artwork. Knill provides a structure for the aesthetic analysis; in the four distinct aspects or directions of inquiry he identifies suggesting a sequence of inquiry in this order:

1. The "surface" of the work.
2. The "process" of shaping.
3. The "experience" of doing it.
4. What does the work say? How is it significant? (152)

The responses of the participants were not always in this order, and it was important to honor their individual responses. The structure described by Knill provided me with a guide to explore the aspects of the aesthetic analysis. The aspect, which is not covered by this approach, is the telling of an emerging story. If a story spontaneously emerged during the aesthetic analysis, I listened to it carefully without referring to the guidelines set by Knill. The aesthetic analysis is part of the interview, and the participants knew beforehand from the lay summary and conversations that the interview would be about their personal family history. So it was very likely that memories connected with a family story would surface.

During the aesthetic analysis, it was important for us to remain in the atelier in order to hold our focus on the artwork and the process. Knill states, "Staying in the studio space with the art work during the aesthetic analysis, however, helps us stay decentered … while at the same time honoring the work and the process" (150). Some participants had the impulse to get up and start cleaning up immediately after the art-making. Nevertheless, in order not to disperse the energy of the experience of the art product and the process, I discouraged the participants from this activity as it could break the connection between the art-making and the analysis.

3.3.3 Harvesting

After the aesthetic analysis and a short break, the procedure I followed was to return to the interview space and settle down. I then picked up my questionnaire and repeated the interview questions in a departure from what Knill describes as *harvesting* (156). By returning to the questions, the participants had the opportunity to elaborate on and deepen the responses. We explored to see if the decentering and the aesthetic analysis had triggered any changes or additional comments.

At the end of the interview, the drawings were photographed for the record and, with the consent of the participants, for inclusion in this study. The drawings are the property of the participants and a keepsake of the interview. In the next section of this study I discuss how the themes emerged from the collected data.

3.3.4 Thematic Data Analysis

In analyzing the data, I looked for *rote Faden* [*connecting thread*], for similarities and contrasts and for the commonalities, which weave through the literature, interviews, field log, and diary.

How could I get a sense of the emerging themes? The material I collected consisted of voice recordings of the interviews and the aesthetic analysis, published material by the participants, emails, notes I had made during telephone conversations with the participants and during the interviews, field log, personal diary, art works including those created during the study, and the research literature. The initial analysis began to emerge through my reflective writings on the collected material. I was then able to start categorizing the material. Creswell sees the categorizing or coding as a process: "This process consists of moving from the reading and memoing loop into the spiral of the describing, classifying, and interpretation loop. In this loop, code or category (and these terms are interchangeable) formation represents the heart of qualitative data analysis" (151).

Initially I used index cards, file folders, and computer files to organize the material. By translating, rereading, and reflecting upon the data, I looked for commonalities among the people interviewed and also for elements that distinguish them as individuals. Collecting, sorting, writing, and resorting kept the research process moving. However, I think the emerging themes were an act of creativity. I agree with Cresswell who states, "Undeniably, qualitative researchers preserve the unusual and serendipitous, and writers craft each study differently, using analytic procedures that evolve in the field. But I believe that the analysis process conforms to a general contour" (150). What Cresswell describes as a general contour I term a *rote Faden*. These connecting threads guided me through the collected data and led me to identify the themes.

3.4 Subjectivity

During the last year, on and off, I have been writing down my dreams. I decided to use one dream as a metaphor for the dissertation. In this dream, the chest of drawers plays the central role. The painting above shows the image from the dream and was painted with finger-paint, using my left hand, which was very difficult and frustrating, but it helped me to retrieve the image.
In my dream, though the reason is not clear, I have to leave my home or the place where I am staying. As I get my stuff together, I empty out a chest of drawers. I notice there are too many articles of clothing to fit into my luggage. They are not folded but just stuffed into the drawers. I am unsure what to do; I take what I can in two bags.

This dream came to my mind when I looked at the material for this study. There is just too much material for the dissertation, and it is all unsorted. I have been writing and reading and collecting material for some years now. What are the deeper issues that made me want to write a dissertation specifically related to the theme of descendants of Euthanasia victims? In what way I am a victim of circumstance in my life? To rephrase Atkins: How can this dream be helpful for this study and for my imagination, and how can I access information which goes past my conscious mind (5)?

When I look at this painting, I remember another painting I did. In 2005, when I first considered writing the dissertation, I painted a picture of horror and helplessness: red and black bold strokes of acrylic paint depicting a photo of the killing institution of Hadamar and the crematorium with its smoke stacks where the murder victims were cremated. My own long-held sense of victimhood and experiences in my immediate family had led me to examine our family history intently for the source of this feeling. I began researching the life of my aunt Anna and how her fate as a Euthanasia victim had influenced my life and the life of my family. The painting was the beginning of the qualifying paper for this study, and art-making was part of the process to come close to the subject of Euthanasia.

The Multiple Roles of the Researcher

As a family member of a Euthanasia victim, I am a participant in this study as well as the recorder of the experiences of the other participants. When I re-tell the participants' stories, I shift my position as a researcher according to my bias. My roles also shift between that of descendant and researcher and/or a participant. As the daughter of perpetrator from the first generation and also as the niece of a victim, I feel connected to victim and perpetrator roles. Figure 1 shows this shift in the roles of the researcher.

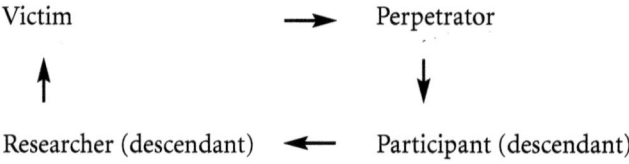

Figure 1: Researcher's Role Shift

Like Clark, I have to remind myself that these roles are contextually sensitive and perpetually shifting—an awareness and response I have come to connect with my dual and sometimes incongruent roles of descendant of a perpetrator and descendant of a victim (9).

4.0 FINDINGS

Consistent with the practice of qualitative research, I offer thick, rich descriptions of the participants in the study; and in order to speak of the participants, I first introduce the Euthanasia victims. The knowledge I have of the victims' lives emerged from stories told by the participants in the research project, from patient files, or official government documents. In presenting portraits of the participants, I have incorporated biographical data, my personal reflection on each participant, and data from the interviews.

The themes which emerged from the interviews, field book, diaries, art work, and the coding of the data, are summarized under the following headings:
- Passing on the intergenerational trauma.
- Present day quality of life.
- Decentering as a research strategy
- Researcher's Experience

4.1 Victims of Euthanasia during the Nazi Regime

Shadowland: Experiencing the Holocaust Memorial

When I look at the Holocaust monument in Berlin, a memorial to the six million Jews of Europe who were murdered during the Nazi regime, the scale and context are as imposing as the Brandenburg Gate, which was built to celebrate war victories. The Holocaust monument commemorates the atrocities during the National Socialist regime in Germany. The vastness of the monument conveys the huge, devastating scale of the Holocaust, while its physicality shows the impact of the Holocaust on our lives today. I feel the impact now, even on the children who run in between the columns and play hide and seek. Watching the children, I see them getting lost, not finding their playmates again, a scary experience. I keep my eyes on the horizon, in order not to lose myself in the jungle of these columns.

It is a sunny day and tourists are sitting on the low columns on the perimeter of the monument, stopping to take a rest. Shadows paint sharp black and white contrasts on the light grey concrete steles and the pathway in between. There is something, which draws me in to walk between the columns, and yet I am hesitant. I look around to orient myself; the rectangular blocks of concrete on the outer rim of the area are low, barely rising above the ground. I start to walk into the interior of the field of columns and notice that the columns are getting taller. As they get higher, the ground starts to become uneven. The ground rises and falls in gentle waves. The paths are covered with small square stones, which remind me of the "Stolpersteine." I have to watch where I tread so as not to stumble. The light and shadows, the uneven ground, and the looming columns are confusing and frightening. I feel as if the tall columns on both sides of the narrow corridor are closing in on me. When the monument was built, the columns were perfectly aligned. Now some of them lean to one side due to the ground settling. I scan the horizon of trees and apartment buildings skirting the monument. In my imagination I see the descendants of the Euthanasia victims walking a land of shadows, tall columns, and uneven ground. If there were not this glaring unpleasant sharp light, there would not be the deep, dark shadows. Light and shadow provide a metaphor. The perpetrators, the Nazi criminals stand in the glaring light, while the victims, for the longest time, hide in the shadows.

The Euthanasia victims in this study were people who died at the following psychiatric hospitals in Germany: the *Badische Heil-und Pflegeanstalt Emmendingen* [the Baden Sanitorium and Nursing Home, Emmendingen], the *Landesheilanstalt Hadamar* [the State Sanitorium, Hadamar], and the *Landes-Pflegeanstalt Grafeneck* [State Sanitorium, Grafeneck].

Karl Schreiber: A Loving Father
Most of Karl Schreiber's portrait is from his patient files. Günter Schreiber, his son and a participant of this study, remembered very little about his father. He was five years old when Karl Schreiber died. Günter has loving memories towards his father as he writes in a letter to the mayor of Freiburg recounting his family story. Karl Schreiber was born on April 28, 1904, in Freiburg, Germany. He was married and had four children. He died under suspicious circumstances at the *Badische Heil- und Pflegeanstalt Emmendingen* on July 21, 1941. In the Landesarchiv Baden-Württemberg, Staatsarchiv Freiburg, are the following excerpts from a patient file at the *Badische Heil-und Pflegeanstalt Emmendingen* in 1938:

"Karl Schreiber experienced a nervous breakdown in 1930 and was unable to go to work. During his illness he experienced a revelation. He felt that he was a "child of God" and that the devil came to him at night with much noise. He was admitted the first time to the *Psychiatrische und Nervenklinik der Universität Freiburg i. Breisgau* [Psychiatric and Neurological University Clinic of Freiburg in Breisgau] in 1931. Then [he was admitted] again for short periods in 1935, 1936 and 1938. ... the personality of the patient changed over time ... The way he behaved point to [the diagnosis of] schizophrenia."

In the medical records of Landesarchiv Baden-Württemberg, Staatsarchiv Freiburg, Bestand: E 120/1 Karl Schreiber, Psychiatrische und Nervenklinik der Universität Freiburg i. Breisgau is also a statement by his wife:

"He (Karl Schreiber) was always healthy ... He has now been without work since eight weeks. He is feeling ill and spends most of his time in bed. He is not really in any pain apart from headaches which he has had his whole life. For three days he has been suffering from severe stomach ache. At times he cries out because of the pains, so much that he frightens the neighborhood. Yesterday he had a fit of rage during which he broke his chair. He has never had such or similar fits. Mr. Schreiber has always been very religious ..."

Another document in his patient file reads thus: Karl Schreiber was admitted to the *Badische Heil-und Pflegeanstalt Emmendingen* in 1935 for the first time diagnosed with schizophrenia and having committed the crime of destroying his military identity card.

At some time during one of his stays in Emmendingen, Karl Schreiber had a vasectomy and spent time at a rehabilitation clinic. His daughter, who visited him the day before he died, told her cousin that her father was a victim of medical experiments. His daughter entered the hospital without permission from the warden and noticed a cart with surgical instruments next to her father's bed. He was not capable of speaking to her anymore before he died. When his wife came to the hospital the next day, she insisted that the coffin should be opened. She saw black marks on his body and concluded that he had been poisoned. Klee recounts in detail an eyewitness's recollection of the poisoning of patients, "Some of these patients also foamed at the mouth, as is the case with epileptics, and their faces turned blue. Once I saw five or six male patients lying in a row, turning blue and gasping for air" (436).

Karoline F: A Servant to Rich Farmers

Karoline F. (pseudonym) was born August 9, 1895, in a small village nestled into a low mountain range in the middle of Germany. The family members also referred to Karoline as "Lina." She was the oldest of six children: four boys and two girls. Karoline F. attended the village school until age fourteen when she was also confirmed in the Protestant religious tradition. After Karoline F.'s confirmation, she became a servant to a rich farmer. In 1917 she changed her place of employment in order to be near her hometown. Beate Schneider, Karoline's great niece, researched the life of Karoline. She narrated from the interviews with Karoline F.'s relatives:

> "She had a difficult time in Neudorf."
> "She only had old, mildewed bread to eat."
> "She did not get her period."
> "She had a boyfriend, but they broke up."

Karoline F. went back to her family before the year was over. She was under constant surveillance by family members as she had tried to commit suicide, crawling into the oven on several occasions and once jumping into the well. Later that year she was admitted to the *Heil-und Pflegeanstalt Andernach*. Her patient file from Andernach is missing; and Dr. Krüger, the clinical director of the *Landes Nervenklinik Andernach* [State Neurological Clinic, Andernach] stated in 1993 that schizophrenia was the probable cause of her admittance.

On May 8, 1941, Karoline F. was transported with 89 other patients from Andernach to the *Landesheilanstalt Hadamar*. She was killed on the same day in the gas chamber. Karoline F. died three months after Anna Gerecht, whose descendants I also interviewed for this study, at the same killing institution.

Katharina V.: A Well-liked and Kind Person

Katharina V. (pseudonym) was born 1898 in Lahr and murdered on November 26, 1940, while a patient of the Badische *Heil- und Pflegeanstalt Emmendingen*. Katharina V. was married and had two children. "She was a kind, well-liked person," the daughter of a midwife told Gardy Ruder, Katharina V.'s granddaughter and participant in the study.

Katharina V. suffered from "mood swings" following the birth of her two children. After the birth of her first son, she was admitted to the hospital in Lahr; and she spent six months at the *Heil- und Pflegeanstalt Illmenau*. Two years after the birth of her second son, she spent four months in the *Badische Heil- und Pflegeanstalt Emmendingen*.

During her last extended stay at the *Heil- und Pflegeanstalt Emmendingen* from July 1932 until November 26, 1940, her husband divorced her, mainly for economic reasons. One year after the divorce in 1934, he remarried. Delius writes that the family members and the patients grew apart, not only through long-term physical separation and the restrictive rules of the hospitals but also through the practice of destabilizing families by simplifying divorce procedures. Further, "a beautiful death for some, relief for others, salvation for both" (65) made sense.

According to her granddaughter Gardy Ruder, Katharina V. had no way of returning to her children and family and no place outside the psychiatric hospital to go. Four years after her second admission, her health improved and stabilized. Katharina V. asked her family of origin to help her to find a place to live outside the hospital, but there was no possibility for the family to support her.

On November 26, 1940, Katharina V. was transported from the *Badische Heil- und Pflegeanstalt Emmendingen* to the *Landes-Pflegeanstalt Grafeneck*. Gardy Ruder stated that Katharina V. died in the gas chamber in Grafeneck, humiliated, degraded and deprived of her rights.

Anna Gerecht: No Ashes, No Grave

Anna Gerecht was born on October 4, 1911, in Bad Homburg. She was killed in the gas chamber of the *Heil- und Pflegeanstalt Hadamar* on February 13, 1941. She was 29 years old. Anna Gerecht was my aunt and my father's youngest sister.

Anna was the second child of Josef Franz Gerecht and Maria Gerecht. Her father was the sexton at the city's Catholic Church and operated a store selling devotional items. Her mother, who married at the age of 20, was a housewife who also worked at the store. Anna's parents died at a very young age, her father dying at the age of 42 years and her mother one year later at the age of 32. According to my father, a possible cause of their parents' death could have been tuberculosis.

At some time during her early childhood, Anna contracted meningitis, an infection of the brain, triggered by bacteria or a virus. It can lead to severe brain damage, which seemed to have been the case with Anna.

I assume that Anna stayed in the family until her parents' death, but it is not known where she spent the years between 1922 and 1935. In 1935 at the age of 24 years, Anna was admitted to the psychiatric hospital in the town of Herborn. She was registered in Herborn from August 3, 1935, until her deportation to Hadamar. The records at the city of Herborn give the date of deportation as February 3, 1941.

Anna and 71 other patients were transported from the psychiatric hospital in Herborn to the *Landesheilanstalt Hadamar* in grey buses. Anna died the same day in the gas chamber of carbon monoxide poisoning. Lifton describes the procedures as follows:

"After doors were closed, the air was sucked out of the gas chamber through a ventilator operated by the same doctor who carried out the earlier "examination". Then for about ten minutes carbon monoxide was let in (by that doctor) and its effect observed through a small window. As soon as he thought that those shut in had died, he had the gas chamber emptied … However the great majority of corpses were immediately taken to the ovens and burned there." (73)

The search for Anna's remains has so far been unsuccessful. There is no grave for Anna. There is no record with either the city or the cemetery administration of her hometown, Bad Homburg, or a record that her remains are buried at the graveyard of the *Heil- und Pflegeanstalt Hadamar*.

In a letter from February 9, 2005, Dr. Lilienthal, Director of the memorial site of Hadamar, confirmed that Anna Gerecht on February 13, 1941, was transported from Herborn to Hadamar. He writes: "Normally, the patients from a typical transport like this were sent to the gas chambers in the basement of the hospital and murdered [in the gas chamber] the same day."

For legal reasons, the city of Hadamar refuses to issue a death certificate, just as the city of Bad Homburg refuses to issue a birth certificate or to release information regarding the towns and addresses where Anna could have been registered.

4.2 Portraits of the Participants

The portraits describe women and men, descendants of Euthanasia victims, whose stories serve prominently in the discussion of the findings that follows this section. In the methodology section, I explained how I met the participants. It is not only their relationship to the Euthanasia victim and the order of birth, which influence the lives of the descendants, but also the era into which they are born. The Nazi regime, World War II, and the post-war years of building a democratic country also shaped the lives of the participants in a significant way.

The following six biographical portraits are not chronological vitas, but are my subjective view of the participants colored by our relationship. The context of the descriptive portraits is the interviews, emails, and phone conversations and the interviews sites.

The participants kindly invited me into their homes where we carried out the interviews. With a curious architect's and artist's eye, I scanned the layout of their home environment, trying to get an overall view. I specifically connected with the artistic and aesthetic expression of the participants as reflected in their environment, something I can appreciate.

Günter Schreiber: An Artist of Life

I walk up to the third floor of a low-income high rise, an assisted-living facility operated by a non-profit organization. The building's entrance door with its wired glass panels looks well used. The dark hallway with bland, beige walls and wooden handrails on both sides lead to his apartment. A bicycle leans against the wall in front of his door.

Günter Schreiber is a very tall man, over six feet, wearing beige designer jeans and sneakers. A sweater is slung over his wide shoulders. After introducing myself and handing him the cake I have brought with me, I am ushered into the apartment by Günter.

Günter gives me a guided tour through his studio apartment; the wall above a large flat-screen TV is covered with a collection of postcard-sized renderings of Günter Schreiber's drawings. The images are of the city of Freiburg, parks, and visionary drawings of his dream house in Brazil. Lining the opposite wall is a huge cupboard typical of German living-room furniture of the 1950s and 1960s. Behind glass doors a book with the title: *Die Hitlerzeit 1933* ... (*The Time of Hitler 1933* ...) is on display.

In the kitchen a wall opposite the L-shaped cupboards is decorated with a wooden carving showing a coat of arms. His collection of drawings and sculptures and his electric piano seem to reflect his life as an artist–artisan and his love for music. Between the kitchen and dining area stands a small desk with an old-fashioned typewriter where a piece of paper partly typed waits to be used again. Günter is writing his memoirs.

Günter's childhood was marked by his father's illness and by his being a wartime refugee. The end of the Nazi regime and World War II marked his early adulthood. At this time, he entered the workforce where he encountered violence from his colleagues; some of them returned prisoners of war.

Born in 1936, Günter Schreiber was the son of Karl Schreiber, a clerk, and Helene Schreiber, a housewife. He grew up with his two brothers and a sister in Freiburg and in a small village in the Alsace region of France. Günter was five years old when his father died. After his father's death, his mother brought Günter and his brothers to a Mennonite family in France. A social welfare agency in Freiburg had threatened the brothers with forced sterilization if the family wanted to receive social security. Günter told me of his childhood in France: "I had a very happy childhood in France. There were no fights in the family. Every member had to do an assigned task." Günter's work was cleaning the shoes of the family. He did not mention where his sister spent the war years.

The illness of his father had begun before Günter's birth. It must have been difficult for Günter, growing up without a father most of the time and without a mother some of the time. Growing up without a father seems to have been passed on to the next generation. Günter's son too, felt that he grew up without a father, a fact he told me in a telephone conversation.

Today, Günter is married to his fourth wife. In his previous marriages there were major problems with infidelity and alcohol abuse and fraud. I could hear the sadness in Günter Schreiber's voice. When I talked to him on the phone I noticed his voice: It was without expression. He seemed to have taken on the sadness of his mother. "She was always sad, sad, sad," he told me in the interview. Günter indicated that he had a close relationship with his mother. He supported her financially throughout his adulthood and protected her from his brother who became violent towards her. Günter intervened to rescue his mother and called the family doctor so that the brother could be admitted to the psychiatric hospital. He recounts that both his brothers were violent and spent time at the psychiatric hospital. One of the brothers seemed to have suffered from paranoia.

I see Günter as a caring and charming family person who also liked some adventures. He was also brave, defending himself and his mother with physical strength.

His longing for a large, happy family, something like the family life he experienced in his childhood in France, was expressed in his drawing of the family hotel. I think he would have liked to live in Brazil if he had not become ill.

Erika Schneider, Caring for the Family

> After a three-hour drive through a winter barren landscape, I arrive in a large industrial town in the center of Germany, at the home of Erika Schneider. Carrying flowers for Erika and Beate Schneider, I walk down a narrow path that leads from the street to the front door of the duplex. In front of the house is a small fenced-in yard. The house is typical of the 1960s, part of a large residential development for blue-collar workers adjacent to an area of heavy industry.
>
> We conduct the interview in the cozy loft of her house. It is a comfortable place, a family room with mementos of past events.

Erika Schneider points out the rose bouquet, which she kept from her silver wedding anniversary some twenty-five years ago and a large photograph of her youngest daughter adorns a wall on the far side of the room. Behind a couch, decorated with knitted and hand-painted pillows, wall plates are on display.

When I walk into the living room, Erika is resting on the couch wearing her dove-blue, hand-knitted two-piece outfit. She says: "I am wearing it today, because I don't go out so often anymore." She seemed comfortable receiving a stranger while reclining on her couch. Her informality in turn made me feel immediately welcome. Her son-in-law and her husband, who sits next to a round dining table, flanked her on both sides of the couch.

Erika Schneider (pseudonym) is a second-generation descendant of a Euthanasia victim, the niece of Karoline F. She was born in 1935 and grew up in a mountainous rural area of Germany with a harsh climate. Her parents were farmers. She is married and has three children. For most of her adult life, she has stayed at home and cared for the children and the household.

Erika was six years old in 1941, the year Karoline F., her aunt, was murdered. She states in the interview that during her childhood the family did not talk about her Aunt Karoline. She did not feel a connection to Karoline until her daughter Beate started to research into the life of Karoline F.

Erika is a caring and compassionate woman. The family, her church, her garden, and knitting are important to her. She and her daughter Beate, support each other in the research into the life of their aunt and great aunt. Some years before, Erika and Beate made a stand against alcoholism in the family. Erika is concerned about her son, worrying about his future. "His life is not so easy," she said in the interview. She acknowledged that her son is sensitive and easily offended. Erika speaks about caring for her mother during the last years before her death. "My mother was ninety-four years old. I had the honor to care for her during her last one and half years." Erika is open to discussing problems in the family and tries to be part of the solution.

She treats her artwork with as much attention to the detail she shows in the care she takes of her family. She remembered a picture she drew in her son's rehabilitation clinic, the family sitting around a table. Now she misses her boy coming around on the weekend to get some cake.

Being in Erika Schneider's home, I feel like I am going back in time. During the coffee break between the interviews, Erika serves traditional German cakes. After the interviews we eat supper together, tea and cold cuts, which I know so well from my childhood.

Beate Schneider, Environmental Activist and Pioneer

> When I arrive at her mother's home, Beate opens the door, cell phone in hand, anxiously waiting for me and concerned that I may not find the house. She has a lively, youthful appearance and looks about ten years younger than her age. I notice her short dark hair. She wears a white t-shirt, sweater, and black jeans.

I first met Beate Schneider (pseudonym) together with her mother Erika at a gathering where Beate was representing the families of Euthanasia victims. In the months following the gathering, we were e-mailing and phoning in order to arrange a time for the interview. Beate had a very busy schedule. Finally we found a date which also corresponded with a reunion in her family. She arranged with Erika that we could conduct the interview at Erika's house, Beate's childhood home.

Beate Schneider was born in 1958, the oldest daughter of Erika Schneider. She has a younger sister and brother. She is married without children and is by profession a scientist and owns a consulting business. She is the great-niece of Karoline F.

In 1992 with the help of her mother, Beate took the initiative in carrying out extensive research into the life of her great aunt. For her research, she interviewed family members, specifically asking why they had remained silent and did not talk about Karoline F. She also contacted church registries, psychiatric hospitals, and the local registry office looking for traces of Karoline's existence.

Beate feels very emotional about her great-aunt Lina's fate, as she puts it: "I grieve, and I am speechless. Having uncovered the family secret, I can feel grief and sadness, and yet I must carry on with my life and face new challenges." Beate feels that it is important for her to separate herself from the grief she feels for her great-aunt. She feels a responsibility to herself to lead a fulfilled life despite her grief.

Before we started with the interview, Beate talked about her busy life. I became aware that she speaks very fast. She is proud of her work. If she takes a day off during the week, she feels she has to work on Sundays. There is pride in her voice in being able to work the long hours and evenings, which go along with owning a business, and being successful. "Always too much or too little business," she said, when we shared on the telephone. At the time of our interview, she had also had concerns about her health, which I believe made her feel stressed. I was touched by Beate's trust and by her sharing her concerns with me. Before I left the Schneider's home, Beate handed me a folder with information about Karoline F. and her family.

I am very grateful for her contribution to the study. I experienced Beate as open and trusting. She also is very structured in her daily life. She can separate her life from the victim's tragedy.

Gardy Ruder: I Go My Own Path

>Gardy opens the front door of her home with a warm hello. I notice her long brown hair is bunched together in a ponytail. She wears fur boots, a fur vest, black soft fabric pants, and a long-sleeved T-shirt. After the interview, we go on a tour of her apartment. She points out her healthy houseplants, raised from seeds or given to her. She is especially proud of her gardenia plant, a flower she is named after.

Gardy Ruder is a third generation descendant and the granddaughter of Katharina V. She was born in 1954. Gardy is divorced and has an adult daughter and grandchild. A disability caused her to retire from teaching school at the age of forty-three. She now lives by herself near her parents who are at home in the neighboring village.

Gardy Ruder is an activist who keeps memories of the Holocaust victims alive. She has published the work, *Holocaust im Gedächtnis einer Puppe, Unterwegs auf Lebensspuren von und mit Inge Auerbacher*, the story of Inge Auerbacher, a Holocaust survivor. She initiated the Stolpersteine memorials in the town of Lahr and is also active in seeing that memorial plaques are fixed onto houses and buildings where prominent Jewish people lived.

Gardy's relations with her immediate family are difficult. Her parents refused to talk about her grandmother, an issue that is very close to her. She says in the interview: "I don't think they can deal with it. I don't have to prove anything to them, and I don't have to press the issue for them to contemplate because they don't understand." Gardy's heart is with her grandmother.

I complimented Gardy on doing the research into the life of her grandmother while her parents are still alive, something I could not have done. I started my research after both of my parents had passed away: The wall around us was impenetrable. When I wanted to share an issue, which was sensitive to me, I was afraid and expected an angry reaction from my father. When he unexpectedly shared a painful experience from his childhood, I reacted with silence, unprepared to respond to his sudden revealing of an emotional incident.

After the interview, Gardy invited me for lunch, and it was the start of a friendship, which should last for many years. I experienced Gardy as a very thoughtful and serious person. She struggles with her family and still she always reconciles things with them after a disagreement. Gardy sees the value of her family even when they oppose her research into the life of her grandmother.

When I walk into Karl's house, my eyes wander to the photos he exhibits in the small entry foyer, photos from his vacations in Hawaii and Greece. He loves to travel and take photos. Several small clay sculptures that I gave him as a present are sitting on the windowsill in his living room. Karl is my oldest brother. A poster of the artist Christo's installation of the "Berlin Reichstag" is displayed on the wall above the couch. The buffet is still from the time of his marriage to the mother of his daughters. Two towers of CD shelves are framing a stereo system. Nothing much has changed in Karl's home. Since I have visited him over the last 13 years, he has not redecorated his home.

Karl Gerecht, a retired schoolteacher, is a second-generation descendant. Karl was born in 1945, four years after his Aunt Anna Gerecht was murdered in the gas chamber of the *Heil- und Pflegeanstalt Hadamar*. Karl is divorced from the mother of his children. He now lives by himself, which must be challenging after his busy working life surrounded by his students and colleagues. Karl leads a very structured life. He tries to occupy himself by scheduling at least one activity each day, he stated in the interview.

During the interview Karl talks about family ties. He sees his family as an entity and experiences himself as a link in the chain of generations. He states with indignation, "The sister of your father was killed!" He does not say his "aunt." Would that have felt too close? I am surprised when he says after the interview: "Now I have spent two wonderful hours, maybe that sounds funny, but I gained clarity about us [the family] and myself." Karl did not elaborate on his words. It is not easy for him to express his emotions. He and I lead very different lives. Yet we have moments where we feel close to each other.

We both gained some insight about the meaning of the family secret during our interview. Even if there is some knowledge about the family secret, expressing emotions means gaining knowledge and revealing the secret, bit by bit. I am glad that I interviewed Karl, not only to gain valuable insights about family secrets also share our time as brother and sister.

Christine Garden: Juggling Many Tasks

Christine greets me at the front door of the house. With a lively gesture she asks me into the house. Her oval face has a fine ivory complexion. The raised eyebrows give her face the expression of astonishment. Christine has long auburn hair reaching down her back when she wears it open. Today her hair is tied together in a ponytail.

The stairs to the front door of Christine's house are solid sandstone blocks, with a concave indentation in the middle from countless feet going up and down over four generations. Inside the front door the floor of the corridor is tiled with black and white odd-shaped ceramic tiles. I notice the paneled kitchen door with the row of knobs for aprons and the rail for towels, above it green-yellow ruffled glass panes giving some light into the corridor.

Christine and her partner remodeled the kitchen of her grandparents' home together according to their needs. The cabinets have been replaced and so has the wallpaper. We conduct our interview in the kitchen after a meal with her son and her sister, who will baby-sit the boy during the interview. I remember that meals are important in our family and that the tradition is continued to the next generation.

Born in 1976 as the oldest child in a family of three girls, Christine Garden (pseudonym) is the youngest participant in this study. As the great-niece of Anna Gerecht, she is a third generation descendant. She lives with her partner and her young son. Christine is an engineer by profession and also a businesswoman. Until I started my research, Christine had not known about her great-aunt who was killed during the Nazi regime.

It is difficult for Christine to connect with her great-aunt Anna and to see her as part of her family. Christine thinks that if we go to Hadamar together, she will be able to connect to the life of Anna. She feels that she needs some physical evidence to feel and be emotionally touched. She lives in the same town where her grandparents and Anna lived.

I notice that some of the habits seem to stay in the family. Christine walks through the castle park along the same gravel path as her grandmother and her aunt did. She passes through the garden on the way from and to her errands. Like her grandmother, she also combines this pleasant walk with her household shopping. Some habits seem to stay in the family.

I see Christine as a reliable, lovable, and clever person. There are many physical and intellectual aspects in her life that are important to her. She laughs easily and has a strong sense of humor, yet in the next moment she can be serious. She cares for her extended family, and she feels it is her duty not to forget any birthdays. I experience her as empathetic with her mother, despite a difficult relationship.

Christine speaks hesitatingly about her hurt feelings regarding her mother and she is angry with herself that she cannot let go her resentment. She easily puts other people's needs before her own, which than is a burden to her. I sense that her life is not easy, but even in her young age she shows compassion and also acknowledges the need to find time for herself.

4.3 Summary of the Findings, Emerging Themes

In reviewing and reflecting upon the data from the literature, the data from the interviews, and the data from my personal reflections, several major themes emerged. The first theme relates to the intergenerational trauma experienced by the descendants of Euthanasia victims. The second theme relates to the quality of life of the participants. The third theme addresses major findings from the interview process itself and how during the art-making and aesthetic analysis the interview answers deepened and expanded. The last theme I recount my experience as a researcher, how I see myself as a researcher, and in relationship to the participants and how sensory awareness and visual images have enriched my research and the findings.

4.3.1 Passing on the Intergenerational Trauma

Some of the participants of the study remember being brought up in an emotionally cold family environment. As Karl points out in the interview, and the way I experienced my upbringing, our parents worked very hard which did not allow for warmth and celebration. After the World War II with the emphasis on work and building a new society, emotional closeness had a low priority for families and individuals. Gruen points out that it is difficult for anyone who experienced the brutality of the Nazi regime to feel close connections in relationships or experience a sense of belonging (32).

It is difficult to say exactly what the consequences of the Holocaust and the Euthanasia crimes are for the following generations. The passing on of the intergenerational trauma demonstrates the chasm such secrets can cause, both within the families and inside the individual. This chasm can either widen, or it can narrow through talking and emotionally working through the family secret.

When I introduced this study to my family, a family member pointed out in a discussion that she is not only the descendant of a Euthanasia victim but also of many different forbearers. Her comment reminds me that many other events in our society influence the lives of the families.

Chasm, Secrets and Stigma

In my imagination, I see the intergenerational trauma like a chasm, a deep cut between the generations that potentially can separate the family members. This divide is difficult to overcome. Some of the participants in this study have been able to bridge the gap. In some families, the taboo of talking about the Euthanasia victim in the family keeps the gap between the generations open.

A way that intergenerational trauma in families gets passed on is through the family secrets. What helps to keep the secret in place is the need to maintain the appearance of a certain family structure, which has to be held in place in relationship to the outside world and in relationship among the family members. A family's secrets are by definition not widely known or talked about. Erika Schneider, for example, is very upset and talks haltingly in her interview about how her grandparents never mentioned Lina: "She was their daughter! My uncle said Lina had tried to commit suicide that she had jumped into the well … Only after my daughter started researching and wanted to uncover it … I have for the first time [found out more about Lina] …"

Erika further elaborated that her mother was not allowed to visit Lina because her mother was pregnant. Not only did the grandparents try to hide their disabled daughter, they probably experienced a superstition about mentally ill people and the encounter with them being harmful to pregnant women.

Tiedemann has the concept of an "under-articulated phenomenon," something that is seldom uttered but whose existence is significant and influential. He points out that family members are unlikely to be able to express painful emotions and confusion in connection with family secrets. If the family secret is connected with shame which is not expressed directly, the secret is overlaid with guilt, violence, envy and anger (69-78). Tiedemann talks about the connection between shame and secret in the personal story in a therapeutic session. Patients often experience an intensive feeling of shame when they tell a story that they have kept secret for a long time (21).

If the Euthanasia victim in the family is not acknowledged, the trauma will likely continue into the next generation. The impact varies for different families depending on how the family as a whole or the individual family member looks at the trauma. Working through the issue frequently involves acknowledging emotions of shame and rage.

In this study, the trauma of the family secret is connected to the stigma of having a disabled relative. As Dr. Lilienthal pointed out in his speech at the 25th anniversary of the *Gedenkstätte Hadamar*, this stigma is why the descendants are reluctant to speak about the crimes inflicted on their relative. According to Perner, family members who break the taboo often become outcasts (89). At times Gardy Ruder feels somewhat alienated from the rest of the family, her parents in particular, by breaking the taboo of speaking about her grandmother. Gardy emphasizes that she goes her own way, which of course does not help bridge the family chasm. It would be challenging for her to find a way to bridge the gap. This perhaps would mean to be empathetic towards her parents even so she feels rejected by them.

Erika Schneider does not remember the family ever talking about her aunt. During her interview she recalls "There was a picture in the photo album and then it was gone … the thing with my aunt lay dormant for a long time until my daughter went to talk to the family members."

Erika breaks into tears while recounting an experience from her childhood. She recalls in the interview "At this time [during the war] people cried a lot. On Sundays, in mass, the priest read aloud the names of the soldiers killed in war." Delius reflects on how the general population perceived the Euthanasia crimes. The start of the Euthanasia crimes was deliberately post-dated by the Nazi regime to coincide with the start of World War II in order to disguise the crimes as war casualties. Delius comments that the general population was meant to believe that the disabled died as casualties of war and not as the result of atrocious crimes (67). Beate Schneider heard by chance of the existence of her great aunt Lina, the sister of her grandfather. She recounts in her interview that it was mentioned during a family gathering. Beate recalls: "In conversation with my parents and other relatives, it was mentioned that someone reminded my grandfather of Lina. I asked, Who was Lina? … There was silence in the room". Beate continues:

> "Lina went to Andernach and from there she did not return. Nobody knows anything more about her. Only in 1992 I decided to find out what had happened to my great aunt. Until this time, I had let the matter rest. I had not continued to ask. With the support of my mother, I started the research in 1993 and continued in 1994 to learn that my great aunt was a victim of Euthanasia murders."

"We don't know any more and we want it to keep it this way", a relative told her. Beate recounts in her newspaper article that the family members pressured her not to ask the grandmother about Lina as she surely would not be able to cope with questions. Beate Schneider asks at the end of her article: "Why the long silence—out of shame, or were they just overwhelmed?"

Sarva Posey, Chasm, Mixed Media 1997

Breaking the Walls, a Challenging Quest
What keeps the chasm of the intergenerational trauma in place? Günter Schreiber grew up with an absent father and tried to protect his mother who was always sad. Because of her sadness, he never demanded that she talk about his father.

Günter did not explain how he first found out that his father was a Euthanasia victim. From the father's patient file, it appears that he was absent some of the time while Günter was a small child. Günter's father was often unemployed or a patient of the *Badische Heil- und Pflegeanstalt Emmendingen* or the *Psychiatrische und Nervenklinik der Universität Freiburg im Breisgau*. Even before Günter's birth, his father had become ill. Günter recalls:

> "My mother talked, but ... [Günter Schreiber's speech is getting slow, he takes many breaks] at this time, after the war, she did not talk so much. It was more in passing that she mentioned my father. I never demanded [that she talks about his father] because I did not want to mention this topic. I had noticed that she was always sad, sad, sad, sad. Because we never heard about it, it was unfamiliar to us. It is unfortunate."

Her inability to talk within the family about her murdered husband passed to her son.

Karl Gerecht remembers the one sentence he heard from our father: "Anna has been taken away. That is all our dad said. "It was difficult for Karl to answer the question about when and how he heard about Anna's death. First he claimed not to have any memory, and then in a quiet voice, he said that he was totally blocked. My probing made him think and then he remembered a remark that my dad had made: "*Ja, Anna ist weggebracht worden.*" [Yes, Anna has been taken away]. He could not remember a time and place where this sentence was spoken, but he remembered the words. Karl speaks slowly with pauses in between the sentences, "I must say, quite spontaneously, I have no recollection .... It has become really clear now through your work .... I know only since you have told me during a visit or phone calls, something has clicked, oh yes true, there was something there ..."

During the interview, Karl's response to the knowledge that Anna was taken away from the family was very emotional. With a raised voice he continued:

> "You cannot put a person in the dump like a piece of old furniture. It's a human being who was taken away. But no, neither he [our father] had an explanation, nor have I demanded an explanation. Yes, and through your work I thought, that's an important part of my history, uh, which I have not paid any attention to."

There is rage and anger in Karl's voice in his response that Anna was treated so inhumanely. My impression is that through traveling to Hadamar and participating in the interview, his sense of and understanding about what family means to him have changed.

Family secrets are kept in order to hold the family structure in place. Sometimes, a family member or an acquaintance at a family gathering makes an unexpected remark about a person without further explanation. Somehow we cannot force anybody to uncover family secrets. A "double wall" surrounds the family secrets. Bar-On states:

> "Between the two generations there arises a kind of double wall: The parents say nothing, and the children do not ask. And even if one side tries to open a window in the wall, he often looks at the wall of the other. That parents and children are spontaneous and open at the same moment, able to share feelings and mutually accept them, is highly unlikely and therefore such an occurrence is rare. Untold stories are transmitted from one generation to the next more often than stories, which are told" (Hoffnung 33).

Time Can Widen the Chasm

Christine Garden told me in the interview that she does not have any personal feelings toward her great aunt. She grew up not knowing about her. When I asked Christine during the interview when she had heard about her great aunt for the first time, Christine replied:

> "That was … you told me about it … I don't know when we talked the first time about it. It was more in-depth when you were here the last time (the year before the interview I was visiting the family). I think we talked about it. I don't know anymore, maybe sometime during the last two to three years."

I assume Christine must have forgotten that I went to Hadamar some years before. I asked her how she felt about her great aunt being murdered: Anna was murdered 35 years before Christine was born.

We both avoid talking about Anna as a person. We talk about "it." Even as we speak about Anna, we avoid coming too close to her by being emotional, and the Euthanasia crimes. Volkan et al. describe members of a group of German and Israeli psychiatrists preparing for a symposium and that the members of the group talked about "it" instead of using the word Holocaust, "Even here, there was a taboo that the members of our group would not break" (154). I ask Christine and she replies:

> "Well, of course I thought about it and what should I say, it does not touch me personally. But I think if you come the next time and we go to Hadamar together, it will be different. My son will be in the kindergarten. I can make time for sure. It touches me insofar as I think it concerns a human being, and

it is more than an individual destiny. If I were to hear about others in the same situation I would feel the same."

Christine wanted to express the fact that she does not experience any feelings towards her great-aunt as her relative but rather more a general feeling of compassion. She would feel the same towards a stranger. She affirmed that her father never talked about her great aunt Anna and that she does not see a personal connection between herself and Anna. When Christine talks about politics with her friends, the Holocaust is mentioned in the context of the Israel/Palestine conflict. "None of my friends has mentioned there being a Holocaust victim in the family, and of course they would not talk about it if they had a perpetrator in the family. We talk about current events and use these as an occasion to talk about the Holocaust."

> I can comprehend that Christine does not have personal feelings towards her great aunt. I only felt a connection after I intensely researched Anna's life and the circumstances and the crimes connected with the Euthanasia murders.

Bar-On writes about the third generation of Holocaust survivors living in a different society. He feels that the Holocaust is more like a legend than a continuous reality for them. It is not something they have experienced in their own lives (Hoffnung 427).

We talk about 'it'…

We don't talk about
how we cannot imagine
a cruel death,
slowly suffocating,
entangled limbs of
a hundred bodies

we don't talk about
her fear riding the bus
with the darkened windows
towards her death

we talk about "it"
to keep a safe distance
not to be touched by the horrors.

Sarva Posey

Christine is trying to close the chasm in her own family of origin. She is the oldest child and the only family member in contact with her mother. Christine feels a sense of duty towards her mother, perhaps replacing any real feelings of closeness. She finds her mother's demands for care and attention and the emotional absence of her father a strain. Although she works with her father on a daily basis, she did not mention him once in the interview.

Telling the Family Secret, Bridging the Gap

One way participants have responded to the knowledge of being the descendant of a Euthanasia victim is political activism. Another way is to share the knowledge with family members, which can draw the families closer together. The family members use their means to publicize and present their knowledge about the Euthanasia victim, to inform the public of the atrocities performed by the Nazi regime.

Working together to address the issue of Euthanasia in the family can further intergenerational relationships. Such teamwork can help the family to cope with the issue by uncovering details of the life of the victim, making the victim a person, and finally lifting the veil of secrecy. The Schneider family and the Gerecht family emphasized the approach of jointly honoring the victim by visiting the memorial sites together.

It is not easy to bridge the gap. In telling the family secret, one has to be able to face conflicts. An awkward attempt to tell the family secret was made by Gardy Ruder's father. She remembers the incident where her father shared his pain. She reports his saying, "She [his mother] could have pulled herself together." Gardy received his secret feeling of the rage of an abandoned child longing for a mother, unable for his mother to care for him due to her illness, with a lack of understanding.

Gardy could not see the pain her father experienced through the loss of his mother. Gruen explains: "We only can heal when we see and know the pain as our own." (214) It is possible that Gardy's father was not allowed to express his feelings about the loss of his mother when he was a child. So as an adult, it is understandable that he expressed his feelings in a childish way.

When Gardy reported the words of her father, she expressed outrage that her father had expressed his helplessness and emotional pain. At this moment Gardy's father was exposing the family secret by expressing his feelings of being abandoned by his mother. As Perner points out, expressing emotions of loss and anger openly can help a person in a way to regain the lost person (48). However Gardy was not able to bridge the gap by feeling compassion for her father.

Gary Ruder found out about her grandmother from her parents when she inquired about her second name, Käthe. That name seemed to her at odds with her first name, Gardy. Käthe was her grandmother's first name, Gardy recalls during the interview, speaking with hesitation:

> "I found out when I was an adolescent. It is connected with my name Gardy-Käthe. Gardy is such a particularly euphonious name … and to add Käthe to it, although the two names do not quite fit together … and as an adolescent I asked how it had happened that my name was Käthe. I must have been around fourteen or fifteen years old. I always tried to get information. It was difficult for my parents to talk about "the topic," and they did not want to. It was this ambivalence … eventually my mother told me in this way: such people whom Adolf [Hitler] gassed … I never met my grandmother … It was for me a denigration of my grandmother, and thus seems to mean … so as if … she has almost earned her fate."

Gardy called the murder of her grandmother "the topic." "The topic" is the death of her grandmother, which meant it is not talked about with her parents. She avoids naming the brutal murder of her grandmother. Knowledge of the murder seemed to be common among the people of Gardy's village. Even fifteen years after Katharina's death, a village woman's response to Gardy made her aware of the fear that mental illness could be inherited. Gardy said, "And then it was the fear, that I know now ... somebody told me ... when my mother was pregnant ... somebody in the village said: Do you not know who his mother [Gardy's grandmother] was?"

Gardy remembers her mother's fear as well, "Also there was the fear that the illness of the grandmother would manifest itself in my father or me ... and then she lived in the fear that I might resemble my grandmother ... and that is what she did not want under any circumstances."

Gardy identified herself with her grandmother's victimhood until she researched her life. By becoming an activist and researching the life of her grandmother, she at times gained some distance of feeling like a victim herself. She has seen herself victimized over and over throughout her life. She still found the courage to talk in public about her grandmother at the former synagogue in Kippenheim to commemorate the sixtieth anniversary of the day of the murder of Katharina K. "By speaking out in public about this atrocious topic, I give my grandmother her dignity back."

Gardy recognizes that for many years she lived in dependent relationships. Writing and researching about her grandmother and reflecting on her life created a distance from her own suffering. Gardy uses the time after her retirement to research the life of her grandmother. In her book: *Holocaust im Gedächtnis einer Puppe (The Holocaust in the Memory of a Doll)* the dedication reads:

"For my grandmother Katharina, close to me in kind and in essence.

Dear Käthe

> it was granted to us
> to meet each other in this life
> though yours was forcibly extinguished
> and my life has been determined and marked
> by the fear of your disease
> yet I have learned many things through you
> and from your life by following your life's traces
> I was able to gather strength
> to write this book."

Gardy feels that she met her grandmother even though she died fourteen years before she was born.

For some of the participants, bridging the gap involved inquiring deeper into the life and death of their family member. Some of the participants researched in state and church archives and patient files. They talked to other family members and interviewed them in a formal way. Beate Schneider reported that not all family members were interested in working through the family trauma. Some did not join the family pilgrimage to Hadamar.

Summary

Knowledge of being related to the victims of the Euthanasia crimes is not easy to embrace or to share. Participants in this study reacted to this knowledge in different ways. Their reaction depended in part on how they learned the information, in part on how the family as a whole had dealt with the knowledge, and in part on how close or distant the participants felt to the victim and to the family in general. Attempts to deal with the knowledge varied from wishing to keep distant from it to expanding and sharing the knowledge with family members to becoming activists in sharing the knowledge in a public way.

Günter Schreiber learned of the death of his father from his mother but did not want to inquire any further into it. Günter's response was that he seemed to have taken on his mother's sadness.

Erika Schneider was curious about a photo that was absent from a photo album which led to her discovery of the death of her aunt. Forty-five years after Karoline F's. death, inspired by and in cooperation with her own daughter, she challenged authorities, demanding information.

Beate Schneider responded to the silence in the family by researching into the life of her great aunt. She withstood the pressure in the family not to continue the research. Between first gaining the knowledge and embarking on the research, approximately six years passed. Her research led her also to publish newspaper articles and represent the families of the victims at public memorial services for the victims. To rephrase Bar-On the family Schneider activated an intergenerational healing process (429) in that Beate Schneider was able to question limitations set by the family to not ask questions about Lina. Beate was able to address the conflict surrounding the life and death of her great aunt.

Gardy Ruder found out about her grandmother when she inquired about her unusual first name, Käthe. Her parents had given her the murdered grandmother's name, but they have never wanted to talk about her grandmother. In response to this secrecy and after a personal tragedy, Gardy researched the life and death of her grandmother herself. She took her research further and became an activist for Holocaust victims.

Karl Gerecht remembered a short remark by his father. His father mentioned Anna and that she was ill and been taken to Hadamar. Karl then heard again many years later through this research project about the murder of his Aunt Anna. During the interview, he expressed outrage at the injustice done to Anna. His response was a visit to the memorial site in Hadamar with his siblings.

Christine Garden found out the first time through this research project about her great aunt Anna. She could not feel a personal connection to Anna but she felt sadness at the death of Anna, a feeling could be the same regarding the death of a stranger too. She could imagine that her feelings might change once she visits the memorial site.

It seems that the research of the participants was also triggered and inspired by personal misfortunes in their lives. Beate Schneider was at loss about her professional future when she started inquiring about her great-aunt. Gardy Ruder started the inquiry into her grandmother's life after the death of her son and her divorce.

I just heard a sentence when I was a child, without explanation. The knowledge revealed itself slowly in the course of the research. I am challenged with maintaining a personal distance as a researcher and at the same time, as a participant, maintaining closeness to personal feelings. Responding to this taboo in the family took me past my middle age. At this time, I found the courage to break the silence in the family.

Re-search

In the black file folders of the perpetrators
Meticulously dated
At the upper right corner
A small handwritten note 'sterilized'
re-search
the face,
where the pain
is engraved
in the small crevice
between the eye brows
the twitch of the corner of one's mouth.
the sinking feeling in the chest

Sarva Posey

4.3.2 Present Day Quality of Life

It is difficult to know exactly how being a descendant of a Euthanasia victim can impact the quality of life of the descendant. What makes research further difficult is that most of the participants are not only descendants of victims but also descendants of perpetrators and bystanders. Some participants clearly attributed current lifestyle practices as being related to being a descendant; in other cases I must infer some relationship.

Activism: Giving Meaning to One's Life

Most of the participants of this study engage in some form of social activism by caring for the disadvantaged people and for the environment. Activism and being professionally involved are resources the participants use to lead a meaningful and fulfilled life. Erika Schneider and Karl Gerecht are engaged in volunteer work for their church. Beate Schneider is an environmental activist; Gardy Ruder is an activist to keep the memories of the Holocaust and Euthanasia victims alive. Christine Garden works as a volunteer with disabled children and horses in a therapeutic setting.

Beate Schneider recalled that the side effect of her successful research into the family history gave her the confidence to further her own professional life. She reached out and asserted herself. She met people from different agencies and different walks of life and expanded her worldview. She states, "When I did the research about my great aunt, I really went into my fears. Talking to important people gave me confidence. I don't blush so much anymore; I used to be very shy." Meeting people gave her the personal confidence to pursue a meaningful professional career.

It is no coincidence that Beate Schneider is an environmental activist who works professionally and volunteers in the environmental consulting field. Beate Schneider grew up in an area with heavy industry. She remarked, "When I was a child, the air was so polluted and the stench from the nearby factory so penetrating that we could not open the windows in our home." Linden makes a comparison in the last chapter of *Making Stories, Making Selves* between the Holocaust and the destruction of the ecosystem. She takes the analogy of the Holocaust, the destruction of the people, one step further. "My thoughts drift to what has become, for me, a self-evident connection between the reality of genocide in our own and past eras, and the decimation and extinction of thousands of other species by direct human action" (149).

Gardy Ruder lives for the memory of her grandmother and the victims of the Holocaust. She is an activist, struggling with being recognized for her work and also feeling like a victim herself. She devotes a great amount of time to talking publicly about her grandmother. She visits organizations to talk about being an outcast and victimized in her own life.

Karl Gerecht and Christine Garden combine their hobbies with volunteer work. Karl likes to travel and combines his volunteer work in Peru with traveling to South America. During his work life, he was active in a cultural exchange program for students and teachers sponsored by the European Union. Christine combines her love for horses with helping disabled children. Christine grew up riding horses. She is using this skill to work with horses to help disabled children.

My father always volunteered to decorate the church for Advent with a big wreath let down from the ceiling. My mother worked on the wreath for a week. My parents gave generously to the church, even though we were not rich, and we children were raised very simply.

Taking Care of One's Self

Participants have different ways of taking care of themselves. To regenerate from a busy workday, the participants have their own strategies. Some structure their day in order to be able to have some recreational time. Professional and personal life is sometimes intermingled.

This coming summer Erika Schneider is looking forward to travel to Tuscany with the church choir. Her husband will accompany her. It seems that they enjoy their retirement after a life rich with work. After the war, other priorities took precedence like helping during vacations at a relative's farm with the harvesting.

Beate Schneider has a very demanding work life, and structuring her time helps her take care of herself, family, and friends. She shares during the interview that she likes to schedule her free time consciously. She prefers to cook regularly in order to have something substantial to eat and to take a break from her deskwork. In her spare time, she likes to watch television—light, humorous entertainment. She makes dates with friends to go to the movies. When her working day is over, she likes to switch off and relax, she explains during the interview.

During our visit, Günter Schreiber served café au lait in oversized cups, "like in France," he pointed out. He carefully measured the coffee and the water for each cup and heats the milk. He serves the coffee with a grand gesture.

Günter Schreiber is very proud of his work as a carpenter. In his photo album are pictures of his shop, the furniture he made intermingled with photos of family and friends. He is very skilled in using every scrap of wood. He points out that he did not let any wood go to waste. He worked on a wide range of projects from a banister he turned on a lathe to the complete room furnishings with matching wall paneling.

As a young man, on summer mornings, he loved swimming before going to work. He is also the proud owner of a bicycle, and he still goes out for short rides his wife told me; I noticed that his bike is chained to the railing outside his apartment. Today, he loves to be entertained by watching television on his huge flat screen TV. When I asked Günter Schreiber what he watches, he said that one of the things he does to relax is to look at sad stories and dramas, and he loves to watch animal movies. During the interview, he told me about incidences with his animals that he and his family kept. He remembers cuddles with his dog and the pranks of his cat.

Günter Schreiber has a taste for the exotic, and he loves music "from the islands," as he calls it in the interview. He made friends with musicians from the Caribbean islands. With his current wife, he lived some time in Brazil but had to leave the country for health reasons.

Gardy Ruder likes to cook; she started working in an art studio once a week. Gardy sees the beauty in her drawing. She goes for walks and loves to swim in a nearby lake. She likes to care for herself by dressing nicely and sewing her own dresses.

Karl loves to travel, visiting his daughters and their families several times a year as well as going on ski holidays and summer vacations with friends. Our phone conversations circle comfortably around the issues of his vacations and his children. When I used to visit my father, I stayed at his home.

Christine likes to regenerate after a busy day with her partner, son, and her sisters. When she spends all day with people and in the outdoors, she likes to spend time alone to take a bath, read novels, or go for a leisure walk combined with household shopping.

It seems there is no difference in the participants' recreational activities from other populations. Every participant in this study did something to stay fit physically and care for himself or herself emotionally.

Challenges of Current Family Life

Current family life seems to be challenging for many of the participants.

Günter Schreiber is a person who lives much in his memory. He does not talk about his relationship with his wife. I notice when I meet her that she hardly speaks any German, and Günter does not speak her native language. While he talked in detail about his deceased brothers and his mother, he talked very little about his current wife and family. He planned for some years to spend his retirement with his wife and her family in Brazil. He designed a family hotel for his wife's extended family where they could live together. When I commented on the architectural rendering of the family hotel, which was displayed on his living room wall, Günter said:

> "That is the utopian ... that is how it should have been. It would have been beautiful, but it was not meant to be. Next to the house [where he and his wife would live] a hotel is situated. That was my first idea, to involve the whole family ... on the same property and with a swimming pool ... But then I realized hat the family is divided ... I married a woman who has eleven siblings."

The reality of a different culture and climate changed Günter's plans for retirement. Günter and his wife returned to Germany also for health reasons. He explained in the interview that he holds his wife responsible for an accident he had while being in Brazil. He feels sorry for himself and misunderstood. Mitscherlich describes this transforming of feelings of guilt, and shame into self-pity as a *German syndrome* (27).

While talking during the interview about a family gathering in his family of origin, Günter went on to talk about his violent brothers. It seems that his brother beat his mother and then she called on Günter for help. Günter threatened his brother with a beating if he did not leave their mother alone. It was important for Günter to mention that he considers himself a kind person. He said he did not know any other way to express his wish for respect than threatening his brothers. "One could compare him [the brother] with an animal: He kicked in the door. She [his mother] stood behind it; everything was green and blue … and such things .. and then he had to go into the [psychiatric] hospital."

In another incident, Günter described that his younger brother, who was very religious like his father, came to see him because he thought he [Günter's brother] had sinned. "Finally I told him to 'piss off' whereas I should have taken him into my arms", Günter regrets. "I did not beat up on my older brother—only wanted to have his respect. Then I could control him a bit." Günter mentioned in the interview that his daughter, at one point, had sued him for child support [for herself]. She must have been very

> I can relate to the fear and rage of the daughter towards her father. In my teenage years I felt anger and rage towards my father. I felt abandoned by him. He did not support my dreams for my own life. At the end of his life I was able to transform my anger into compassion.
>
> Sarva Posey

angry with her father, who left her and her mother when she was an infant. When his daughter tried to blame him, he said to her, "Look at yourself instead of blaming me." He did not respond to her accusation but tried to shame her for being unable to hold down employment.

During the interview, Gardy Ruder mentions that her mother recently became ill. Gardy was still able to care for her, and show some compassion for her parents. She feels that her parents appreciated her help. Though she is helping her parents, at the time of the interview Gardy has no contact with her daughter. She is upset about her daughter's behavior, an anger she does not explain. She states, "I am not willing to take a step towards a person who acts like this [she does not call her daughter by name] … She is highly respected in her place of work. I have not seen her for a long time." Her pride in her daughter is clearly expressed in her mentioning that her daughter is respected at her place of work. Gardy states that she is positive and that she will have contact again with her daughter in future, but she wants to be treated differently and she expects her daughter to be the one to change. During the interview she often stayed vague in her verbal expression, but in her tone of voice I could hear how upset she is.

When Gardy does not feel supported by her family, her priorities are clear, "I follow my own path," she says. "I do not talk about everything." She feels that her parents do not like her activities concerning the Holocaust and Euthanasia. She explains in the interview that she does not need their permission, but she has feelings of guilt towards her parents when she engages in activities that do not meet their approval.

When I asked Karl Gerecht during the interview about a family celebration in his family of origin, meaning from his childhood, he had difficulties in the beginning with the term "family of origin" in the context of family celebrations. He needed time to think, and he asked for clarifications. After a moment, he remembered his first communion. That was a special day for him. He did not go into details about how this special day was celebrated and why he remembered it: "Good, the first communion, actually that was it. I had the impression that celebrations are not so important. The main thing is to work: everything else is not so important."

Both his parents worked very hard to build up their business after World War II, which left little time for celebrations. Karl feels bitter about not having had a happy, playful childhood. It seems for this reason that today he loves to celebrate his round birthdays by inviting family and friends. On occasions like this he feels appreciated and loved, something he missed in his childhood. His daughters entertain the guests at his parties, play sketches out of his life, and sing his favorite songs.

Karl thinks some more about family gatherings. He continues that he appreciates the small gathering of the previous night where we shared dinner with two other family members.

4.3.3 Impact of the Decentering on the Responses to the Interview Questions

One of the purposes of this study was to explore the impact of using decentering through art-making as an addition to the interview process. Decentering, as described by Eberhart and Knill, is a therapeutic method in expressive arts therapy in which the client leaves his/her everyday experience and enters the world of imagination through a special approach to art-making. Through a careful analysis of the process and product of the art-making experience, resources are identified and insight is gained to bring back to the everyday situation (123-135).

In my adaptation of the decentering method for the interview protocol, I used the general method of decentering through art-making. However, I adapted the specific procedures to focus upon eliciting further information appropriate to the research rather than focusing on eliciting resources to address the presenting problem, as would be the case in a therapeutic situation.

In this study, the responses of the participants demonstrated that decentering through art-making served to elicit additional valuable information beyond that which was shared prior to the art-making. The review of the decentering experiences with each participant and my reflections upon each person's responses show the efficacy of this method as an adjunct to the interview process.

I used elements of Knill's and Eberhart's methods of aesthetic analysis and harvesting and have adapted their method to the way I see the aesthetics description of the art product as a visual artist. I used whatever came from the participant's description of surface elements—commenting on the colors and shapes, metaphors, and expression of emotions—or remembered stories which either emerged from nowhere out of the silence of the moment or remembered details that deepened and expanded the answers to the interview questions.

During the harvesting, I read the questions back to the participants without probing for additional information, but I used this time for the participant to add to the questions and to let surprises and additional information emerge.

I describe in section 3.2.2. how I introduced the participants to the drawing material and I demonstrated a possible start to their artwork. A short relaxation exercise helped them to focus on the task ahead. I asked them to welcome any image that wants to surface.

Gunter Schreiber

Aesthetic Analysis

Günter Schreiber used some of his own charcoal sticks for his painting. The picture has black lines that are arranged in different patterns, "V" shapes, cubes with vertical lines, and lines which look like representations of wood grains in technical drawings. The black outlines of the geometric shapes are dominant and in the foreground of the drawing. The colors used are a rich turquoise with some red and brown. A wide blue band stretches across the middle of the page.

A stern-looking man on the right side of the drawing is looking out of the picture. The face is in profile with a black line across his cheek. The man seems to be young with blond curly hair. He wears a padlock covering most of his upper body. "He is carrying a grudge," Günter remarks. His long narrow feet are firmly planted on the ground. Günter remarks that on the left side of the drawing is a curtain with a big box-like shape behind it.

Günter Schreiber states that the blue color represents hope for him. There are five green buds on long stems, still closed, seemingly growing out of the black lines. He states that love is in the background and is hidden by the color black. Günter talks at length about his two-day marriage to his third wife. After the wedding, she left him alone in a hotel and took his money with her. When he met her some days later, he was not able to confront her but had the marriage annulled immediately. I have the impression that it is hard for him to express his shame and anger about this betrayal.

Harvesting

After the aesthetic response, I repeated the questions. There was a change in quality of his answers, for example, to the first question:

> What do you do to relax or for recreation after a workday, and what helps you to cope with your daily life?

The first time, Günter stated that he likes to watch animal movies on TV, dramas, sad stories; and "I like to listen to music, opera or popular music and jazz and Bob Marley—he was a kind of a freedom fighter." I explained the word recreation to him and used the word *hobby* instead. After the decentering, Günter Schreiber answered the question this way: "Hobbies, I did not have any hobbies. This was my work, for example this lion." He points to a sculpture on top of the cupboard ... "Here this ... if I may bother you." He leads me into his kitchen and shows me a carved coat of arms. "This is knotted pine, very soft, with branches, but that does not matter ... and now I will show you my whole story." Günter gets up and brings a photo album. "There I was still young and had long sideburns. This is my shop, this is my wife, and she just arrived ... my first work, only [crafted] with the table saw ... there are works, like this wall paneling, the table I made from old floor planks. In my shop nothing got thrown away."

Günter started talking about his recreational activities before the drawing sequence with watching movies. After the decentering, he talked about what is really important to him: his work and his art. In his photo albums, pictures of himself, his family, and his work are intermingled. He is obviously proud of his projects. I can sense that like many artists and artisans, he does not divide his life between working and recreation. Before the decentering phase, Günter Schreiber could not answer the second question about what he likes and dislikes about himself, but afterwards there was a change.

> What do you like about yourself and what don't you like about yourself? When somebody treats you unjustly, how do you respond? Can you describe a situation in which you were treated unjustly?

Günter talked at length about things in his life that made him discontented. He talked about the abuse he suffered and how his older colleagues mistreated him during his apprenticeship starting after World War II, his violent brothers and his failed marriages. Günter could not think about something he likes about himself. After the decentering, Günter stated, "Discontent, we already talked about it ... what I like about myself, is when I accomplished something, in my profession ... and I see the piece of furniture, I made it, it is such a joy. It was my dream, even as a child, to become a carpenter."

Researcher's Reflections
Looking at Günter Schreiber's picture I feel harshness, hard lines, few round shapes. His wives have no names. He refers to them by numbers or country of origin. I feel uneasy when he talks about his resentments; I sense he is covering his feelings of shame and anger by claiming that he is a nice person.

The drawing reminds me of the drawings of a landscape and of buildings which grace the living room walls. I admired his art when I first came to his home. The drawing technique he used during our interview is similar to his other art works. I sense his pride in his accomplishments.

Erika Schneider

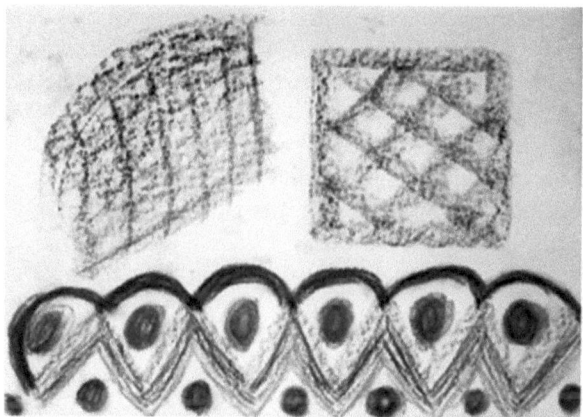

Aesthetic Analysis

There are three distinct elements in Erika Schneider's drawing. She called the largest element, which extends across the bottom of the page, a pattern for knitting a tablecloth. In the upper left corner is a rectangular patch with green and blue areas and thin red vertical lines. Erika explained that it was sky and rain, sometimes rain and sometimes sun. A blue-framed square in the upper right corner with red and green diagonals represents darning or weaving. The three elements of the drawing each have a distinct pattern and are not connected. They represent her hobby, knitting, but also her emotions, tears, and laughter and her everyday life represented by darning.

Erika experienced the process of drawing as freeing and playful. She tells that the only other time she had painted as an adult was at a family day in the rehabilitation clinic where her son was recovering from alcohol abuse.

Harvesting

Being free and playful, she was also free to remember spontaneously a situation and re-experience the grief and shame of being harassed while working as a seamstress. Erika Schneider gave the answer below to the question:

> What is it about yourself that pleases you, and what causes displeasure? When somebody treats you unjustly, how do you respond? Can you describe a situation in which you were treated unjustly?

"I remember something you asked me about being treated unfairly. I was a seamstress, only work, work, and work. The boss's girlfriend, his future wife, treated me unfairly. She was arrogant. Even though I only had a part-time job, I always worked longer hours, no lunch break. I asked for a raise, but it was denied. I was being harassed, and in the end I became ill with a trigeminal neuralgia."

Erika then decided to go to a rehabilitation center and not to go back to work: "After the rehabilitation stay I was unemployed, went on the dole, and because I was married, I felt I was protected. While I was at the rehabilitation facility, the owner called and wanted me to come back to work."

Erika Schneider was proud that she had refused to go back to an abusive situation. She does not seem to bear any resentment against her former employer now. One of her daughters later became an apprentice at the same company.

Researcher's Reflections

After the drawing sequence, in the interval between the end of the drawing session and returning to the interview questions, Erika Schneider spontaneously remembered a situation where she was shamed and harassed. She was treated unfairly at her work place. It seems that doing something she enjoyed, designing a new knitting pattern, gave her the strength to remember a situation where she was treated unjustly. The part of the drawing, which shows a knitting pattern, takes up a large section of her picture.

It seems a balanced life style helps her to cope with the difficulties in life. Her love for the crafts is evident and shows in the artifacts displayed throughout her home. Her attitude towards life is expressed in what she called a section of her drawing: "Sometimes rain, sometimes sun."

Beate Schneider

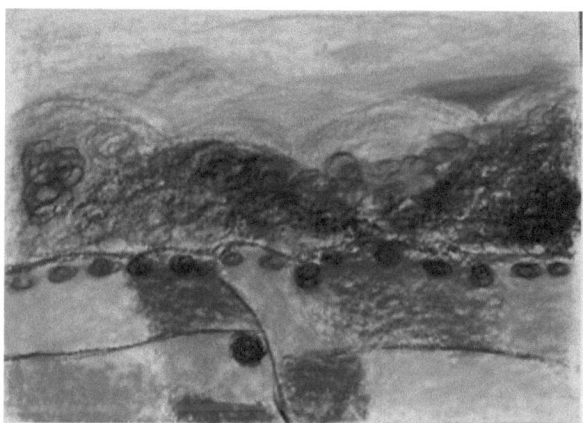

Aesthetic Analysis

In Beate Schneider's drawing, the colors of reddish-brown, shades of green, and yellow-orange dominate. At the top of the picture is a blue area with a small patch of grey. In the upper right-hand corner of the picture is what she calls a setting sun. Beate Schneider's drawing depicts a landscape with rich brown fields in autumn, green hills, and a setting sun, a landscape where she feels safe, she said. Running horizontally across the center of the picture is a stream, according to Beate's explanation, a very thin blue line in contrast to the rich warm green and brown colors. Green foliage or bushes grow on the banks of the stream.

Beate Schneider remembers family vacations as a child, playing with her cousins in the stream, looking for things to find. Her parents, in the meanwhile, helped with the harvest at a relative's farm. Now the harvest is over. She called her painting "Landscape in Autumn." When Beate Schneider described the scene, I felt a tenderness emerging in her. Her speech was slow and soft in contrast to the businesslike, fast-talking woman she had been previously. Her memory of a time gone by seemed to soften her emotionally.

Harvesting

After the decentering, Beate Schneider and I took a break, got up from our chairs, and stretched. We stood in front of the window to gaze at the factory chimneys across the street with their billowing smoke clouds she remembers from her childhood. We returned only briefly to the questions after the break. When I repeated the questions, Beate had nothing to add to her previous answers.

Researcher's Reflections

In the beginning of the interview Beate Schneider talked at length about being very busy. It was challenging for her to find a time for the interview. When I talked to her at the end of December, her busy schedule made it difficult to get a date set for the middle of February. Her heavy workload and not being well hardly allowed her a break. The moment standing at the window, a time without illness and work, just remembering herself and her sister also standing by the window, differed.

Standing there with Beate Schneider, I had a sense of being back in time in her childhood with her. At this moment I felt close to Beate Schneider. The interview felt complete, even though there was no elaboration after the decentering.

Gardy Ruder

Aesthetic Analysis

We recorded the aesthetic analysis during a time when Gardy was visiting me at my home in the Black Forest. I omitted to record our talk during the interview, and after the art-making. Gardy's drawing is very lively, full of movement with a clearly delineated center encompassing colorful shapes. She points to the center of the drawing:

> "The center [of the drawing] I find interesting. It has borders on three sides and an opening on the side to ensure transparency … It is protected but not close. Inside is movement and growth. The green reminds me of plants. I repotted my plants yesterday, and my apartment is getting greener. There is much change [the repotting of the plants] in my apartment and also in my inner life.
>
> At the top in the center of the picture is the blue eye of my grandmother protecting me from the destructive effects of the sand storm in the upper right corner of the picture. The eye of the grandmother seems to be placed between the sand storm and the tulip."

Gardy went on to talk about her grandmother and talked about an incident where a woman remembered her grandmother kindly. The midwife who helped to give birth to her father and his brother appreciated Gardy's grandmother. While Gardy told the story of her grandmother and talked about the different parts of her drawing, emotions came up for her, anger and also joy. She was resentful and angry of people who do not understand her personally and the effect the Euthanasia crimes and the Holocaust has had on her life. While Gardy talked about her drawing, I had the impression that the painting talked back to her. I remember McNiff talking about looking with fondness at the artwork and reflecting on it and letting the artwork speak. He compares this interaction to being in a meditative state (97).

The intense inquiry into the process and product of the painting and the associations, which emerge, creates an alternative world inside the alternative world experience of decentering. When I use the term meditation in the context of the decentering, the term is meant in the sense of thinking about something deeply and carefully. Meditation is a term, which goes deeper than reflection. The drawing, the process and the product activate my own process as a researcher and participant.

Harvesting

After the decentering, we changed places, and went back to sit at the table where we conducted the interview. As in Günter Schreiber's interview, there was a change in the quality of Gardy's answers to several interview questions.

> What do you do to relax or for recreation after a work day, and what helps you to cope with your daily life?

In the beginning of the interview, Gardy talked about how she takes care of herself, structuring her day consciously with going for walks, swimming in summer, and taking care of her cat. She sees her engagement in being an activist as a way to cope with her own challenges in life. Gardy compares the life of her grandmother as a victim with her own life's challenge of being victimized in her profession.

After the decentering in response to the same question, Gardy talked in a small voice about missing an exchange of ideas with other people. She considers herself a loner and likes to walk at her own speed, while at the same time she misses a partner with whom she can exchange ideas.

In response to the second question:

> What do you like, and what do you dislike about yourself? When you are treated unfairly, how do you react? Can you describe a situation where you were treated unfairly?

Gardy felt treated unfairly in her attempts to work in school with projects around the Holocaust. She does not feel valued for her volunteer work. She feels misunderstood by the school authorities and humiliated and excluded by society. After the decentering, asked whether she could remember a situation where she had gained some distance to being treated unfairly, she said:

> "Until some time ago, I was not in a position to respond spontaneously to people [when treated unfairly] to say that I do not find it OK being treated in that way. Meanwhile, let's say, if I am in a good mood, it is easier to answer, that I don't have an overpowering feeling of helplessness … I learn and practice."

In answer to the third question,

> Could you please describe a family party, birthday or Christmas holiday in your family of origin? Please describe your family relationships.

Gardy described the guests at her mother's birthday party. She made a drawing of the seating order and talked about some of the guests. She appreciated the uncle who lives in Canada for his honesty and his human manner. Gardy's voice became very soft when she talked about him.

After the decentering in answer to the question about her family relationships, Gardy confessed that she gave up wanting to talk to her parents about her grandmother. She said that despite the disagreements, she cared about her parents emphasizing, "I have my view of things, and they have their view. I go my way. I don't know how long they will be here. It is important not to leave them alone. It is different with my daughter." Gardy described her difficult and painful relationship with her daughter. She hoped that one day she could make up with her again.

In response to the fifth question:

> When and where did you hear for the first time that your grandmother was killed at Grafeneck?

After the decentering, Gardy basically repeated that she had found out that her grandmother had been murdered and that it was not possible for her to talk to her parents about the grandmother. In addition, Gardy remembered the accusations made by her father about her grandmother. She added:

> "Not long ago I talked to my father … we walked together for quite a long time, than we went out for a meal. Then dad started talking about his brother … his older brother … he joined up and died in the war … and, dad argued, his mother should have made more effort to overcome the disease … His

brother went to war voluntarily because he did not get along with his stepmother and now he is dead and he [dad] blames his mother for his brother's death."

Gardy went on to say that her father lived in his projections, and she left him be with his interpretation of his mother's illness.

Researcher's Reflections

With ease, Gardy Ruder talks about her painting, finding metaphors for its elements. I can feel her excitement about being able to express herself in a creative way. In answer to the first question, Gardy also identifies with being a victim, which makes her feel lonely. After the decentering, Gardy expresses her longing to be more in relationship. At the same time, she feels content living alone.

I can see the movements in her picture. I wonder if the grandmother's eye, which is on top of the picture in the middle is not keeping her from developing more of her own life outside her research interests. As she states, "I still feel isolated, not as much as it used to be." The grandmother's eye stands between the flower and the storm cloud. What if there is nothing between the flower and the cloud? Would the cloud destroy the flower or would it play with it or will it just pass? I wonder what the red column means between the eye and the dust cloud. Gardy assigned the color red to femininity. I actually experience her with a strong masculine side. I can sense strength in the strong lines and clearly defined areas, and I feel some unease about the cloud. I can sense a feeling of trust and familiarity between us. Trust is created by the communality of being a descendant of a Euthanasia victim.

Karl Gerecht

Aesthetic Analysis

After the end of the first part of the interview, Karl walked up to his living room window looking into the garden. It is June, and the roses are in bloom. We used his dining room as an atelier and he sat down in his favorite chair from where he could look into his garden. When he sat down, he decided that he was going to draw this garden view. "Now I sit here for the longest time and very often, this is so beautiful—look here! Look here, what a view out of the window. Well I always knew, you know my house and I mean now I realize, it is so beautiful, I have to draw it."

The drawing is kept mostly in pale shades and covers three-quarters of the paper. Blue and green colors are dominant with some red accents. Karl calls his drawing "my daily view out of the window." The blue of the sky takes more than half of the painting. I recognize the rose arbor on the right side of the picture; on the left is a red beech tree, below little red dots across indicating his bed of roses and hydrangeas. "Well, I first considered, well I mean, I don't have to draw it, like it really is. There is more sky in the picture than I actually see; there are also the dark green trees near the *Urselbach* [name of the little stream], which I did not want [to draw]."

The way in which he drew the greenery in his garden reminded me of a green mountain range. Karl mentioned that he did not show the dark green trees near the little brook, which I can see in the distance. I wonder why he did not include the trees; was there something about the darkness?

Harvesting

Karl did not have anything to add to the first question after the decentering. In his response to the second and fourth questions there was a change, however.

Second question:

> What about yourself that pleases you, and what causes displeasure? When somebody treats you unjustly, how do you respond? Can you describe a situation in which you were treated unjustly?

Karl stated before the decentering that he likes his looks. He likes the fact that he is healthy compared with his contemporaries. He can still do all the things he likes to do.

After the decentering he states that he is sensitive to other people and can read the facial expressions of his friends if they are distracted and look absentminded:

> "If I am with somebody, then I am with this person … and I think, maybe it is just in my imagination … I can see it in a face, how somebody opens their eyes, the facial expression, if somebody smiles, or is tense or relaxed, for example."

Karl informed me that he considered himself to be present in relationships, and he could tell if the other person was not present. Karl likes to compare himself. To measure himself with his friends seems to be important for him. During the harvesting he stated in a short sentence that he was dissatisfied with his dissatisfaction and that seems to be a source of unease for him. He is aware of his comparisons.

Karl answers to the third question:

> Could you please describe a family party, birthday or Christmas holiday in your family of origin? Please describe your family relationships.

He talks about how he celebrated his round birthdays and how his children showed their affection and appreciation. He also appreciates small gatherings. He talks about last night and how we talked about essential things in life.

After the decentering, he extended his recollection of a family gathering to the christenings of his grandchildren. His oldest granddaughter was christened in Germany, his grandson in France. That was to honor Karl and the mother of his children who is French. On these occasions his grandchildren were the focus of the family gathering.

Researcher's Reflections

Looking at my comments on the interview, I realize that it is difficult to keep my personal feelings of being Karl's sister separate and concentrate on the interview.

Karl shows some pride in his good looks and that he can be present in relationship. Pride is something he was allowed when he was a child. In grade school he was an "A" student, and his mother was very proud of him. He could not find associations or metaphors for the objects in his drawings. Karl states that his favorite colors are shades of green. There is nothing green in his house. I never saw him in a piece of green clothing.

Christine Garden

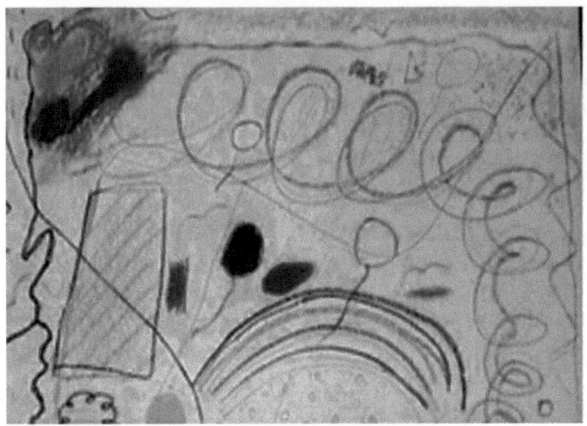

Aesthetic Analysis

Christine calls the picture she drew during the interview, "My colorful life." The drawing is framed in different colors: yellow and blue. On the left side of the drawing, a brown, squiggly line extends to the bottom. In the upper left corner, small blue and magenta areas, the only place that is a little smudged. Green and blue squiggles loop from the upper left corner to the right bottom, and round shapes with strings are attached to them which Christine identified as balloons. They rise from the lower left corner to the upper right corner of the paper. On the left side of the drawing is a yellow field with diagonal green stripes. There are blue lines on the bottom of the paper with a blue *submarine*, as Christine calls it. The blue-colored area on the upper left half of the drawing Christine called sky.

Christine commented that her drawing is colorful, "*schön bunt.*" In the beginning of the drawing session she was afraid of the white and empty piece of paper in front of her. Then, in her own words, she "started to have fun." In a playful way, she could develop one shape after the other. She cannot draw what she calls realistically, which is why she considers herself uncreative. When asked, Christine stated that fuchsia is a cold color; the color is distancing. Orange was the color symbolizing the organizer, a color that provided structure. Christine tried out different techniques and colors and mixing the colors.

When we looked together at her drawing, Christine commented on an area divided and framed in a rectangle. She feels that she is her own prison warden. The warden seems to make sure that she fulfills her duties. Sometimes the demands she places on herself are a burden and make her sensitive and self-critical:

"I am never satisfied with how I look. I take too many things personally; I let myself be touched on a level that is painful. I think much too long about things other people did or said and for sure they have long forgotten it … in the work situation this is unprofessional … It is difficult for me. It is better than it was some time ago, but it is not to my satisfaction."

Harvesting
After the decentering, Christine did not have an addition to the first question. In answer to the second question:

> What is it about yourself that pleases you, and what causes displeasure? When somebody treats you unjustly, how do you respond? Can you describe a situation in which you were treated unjustly?

Like other participants, her response to the second question had changed. Before the decentering, Christine had explained, "I have much love to give; this is important to me. It just pours out of me. I cannot and will not do anything to prevent the love from pouring out." After the decentering, Christine stated:

> "It's stupid when you think about it now, what has been said before. [She laughs a short laugh.] … So I like about myself … uh … I am happy to take care of other people. I think I am, and I am reliable … ehm … This is a positive quality, and it is important to me. I can organize well, for everyday things, every day, but also for a special event, yes."

Before the decentering, she stated in answer to the question the things that she does not like about herself: she takes things too personally, and she does not like her bodyweight. After the decentering, there is new quality to Christine's words about what she did not like about herself. Her answer was more differentiated. She was able to express what was important to her: "What I don't like is that I cannot say no. That is also something I have not considered yet as a concept [to say no?] … and that sometimes I don't take care enough of myself. This is something I did not mention before … It has a lot to do with not being able to say no." She realized that her love of giving and taking care of others had taken its toll on her.

To the second part of the second question Christine responded:

> When somebody treats you unjustly, how do you respond? Can you describe a situation in which you were treated unjustly?

Before the decentering, Christine answered, "I do not feel that I am given the recognition I need. When my mother dumps her anger about my father and my sisters on me, I pretend that I am not listening." Christine tries to ignore her mother's comments. In her response to the same question after the decentering, she admits that she feels a lot of anger and frustration towards her mother. "If it has irritated me, then it just makes me burst out in anger due to distress. That's the way [it is]—when you are angry then you want the confrontation, and you will never get a confrontation from my mother."

Christine answered the question about whether she remembers a family celebration. After the decentering, she recognized the Christmases past as childhood memories, and she misses the joy and excitement she felt as a child. Now as an adult, she has to work in the afternoons on Christmas Eve. She thinks she cannot talk openly anymore at family gatherings; she must consider what she can talk about.

> I feel close to Christine, we are akin. I feel a familiarity in her expres-sions and how she thinks and feels. I am familiar with her home, which I know from my childhood. I am practicing backyard research in the true sense of the word.

4.3.4 Conclusions on Using Decentering as a Research Method

The conclusions made in this section concern only the decentering, which occurred during the interviews. This decentering constitutes of the process and product of the drawings by the participants, aesthetic analysis, and harvesting.

After the art-making and during the aesthetic analysis, Günter Schreiber was able to describe his resentments and his grief. In the harvesting part, he was able to show pride in his workmanship and his projects. A shift in his thinking occurred. He was able to access his emotions, which had previously not been accessible to him.

A surprise occurred after Erika Schneider finished the drawing. In the time gap before the aesthetic analysis, she remembered spontaneously a situation where she had been harassed. The grief she had felt on being harassed in a work situation re-emerged and tears came to her eyes. In this time after working with concentration on her drawing, her painful memory could surface. Doing something creative was a pleasant activity for Erika and gave her the confidence to access painful emotions.

When Beate Schneider talked about her drawing, she recalled playing with her cousins as a child. Childhood memories surfaced in contrast to her busy daily life. After the decentering, Gardy experienced loneliness and also a much needed distancing from being treated unjustly. She recognized that she could now fight back in response to accusations. She also acknowledged and accepted a certain distance to her parents. She was able to feel hurt that her father accused his mother of abandoning him. She is the only participant, which related directly during the interview to the Euthanasia victim in her family.

For Karl, the decentering brought about an opening up of his awareness in that he saw his grandchildren as being the center of attention of a family celebration rather than himself thus acknowledging the value of sharing family time together.

After the decentering, Christine qualified what love and caring means for her. She was able to separate herself from the pleasant childhood memories and acknowledge her responsibilities as an adult.

After the decentering, the answers to the interview questions were more detailed and differentiated. Some of the answers seemed to give space for a different answer to emerge. Drawing also seemed to help to relax the participants so that after the decentering, Günter was able to answer what he liked and disliked about himself. For the first time after Erika finished her drawing she was able to answer to the question of a situation where she felt treated unfairly .

The decentering procedure used in this study echoes again throughout the dissertation in the form of poetry, visual arts, and prose. Poetry and prose passages help to depict and describe feelings, which are normally difficult to express.

4.3.5 Role of the Researcher

Looking back, I notice that my perception of events and people and of myself have changed over the course of this study. In the past, I had a vague feeling that there was something that was affecting my relationships and being in the world, and I could not name the phenomenon. Through retracing the life of Anna, reaching out and talking with members of my own family, contacting other families with Euthanasia victims, I gained insight into how being a descendant of a Euthanasia victim had possibly affected my life.

This realization led me to feel a responsibility for this heritage. As a descendant of a Euthanasia victim, my tendency is to hide and be invisible. The shame of having a disabled relative is greater than the shame of being a descendant of Nazi Germany. As I research the lives of the victims and participants, at times I identify myself strongly with the victim. I feel the shame of being an outcast, a foreigner in my own country. However, at other times, I set myself free to experience the world without this burden of identifying with being a victim. By retracing the victims' lives and with joining fellow descendants and researchers, I find a home.

In aspiring to do the research for this study, I made sure I would care for myself through exercise and meditation, personal writings, being outdoors in natural surroundings, and making art.

Looking Back

> When I look in the rearview mirror of my car, I see the top of my head covered with white hair. Sometimes, when I look in the hallway mirror I have to direct my eyes to look at my shapely legs that carry me through long hospital corridors and hikes in the mountains. My friends sometimes think I walk too fast. My hands are warm and are comforting. I look at the interesting landscape of my skin with marks and wrinkles. I like the fact that I can make faces and laugh about myself. I like to make eye contact with people, which I experience as looking in a different kind of mirror.

I was born in 1950 to Centa and Josef Gerecht, the youngest of their three children with two older brothers. My father gave me the unusual name of *Lucia*, which means the bringer of light. The name was not common in my family. My father owned a plant nursery that had been in the family for three generations. My mother was a Red Cross nurse before she married my father. After her marriage, she was an active business partner in the nursery.

I am divorced without children. I live in a small village in the southwest part of Germany and work as an expressive arts therapist in private practice teaching methods of expressive arts therapy and supervising students in practicum at a university. My therapeutic work extends to being a massage therapist.

I grew up in the post World War II era. For some reason, I was not allowed to play with the children in my neighborhood. I remember looking over the fence watching the girls my age playing with dolls. I can still see the pastel-colored blanket on the grass, and I remember the blankets used in my house—grey, scratchy army blankets. Every day at meal times, we used thick, white dinner plates with the swastika on the bottom. The swastika was used under the Nazi regime as the official emblem of the National Socialist Party. The plates were still good, too good to throw away, my mother said. I am confused about the message my parents tried to convey to us children. I could not see the good in an object with the symbol for the Nazi regime, the evil that killed my aunt and injured my father.

As a child I heard, probably from my mother, that Anna was murdered. My mother never met Anna. My parents married three years after Anna was murdered. The information was short and incorrect: "Anna contracted meningitis and went to Hadamar." That is what my mother told me. The *Heil- und Pflegeanstalt Hadamar* was the killing institution where Anna was murdered after she stayed there less than a day. My mother did not mention that Anna spent many years in the psychiatric hospital of Herborn. I do not know if the family visited her or if there was any correspondence with Anna or the hospital.

I cannot remember that there were any emotions expressed about the fate of Anna. Mother did not explain the circumstances, nor did my father talk about his sister. They did not express any regret that Anna had such a traumatic life and death. Both my parents talked about how hard and difficult their life was during and after the war. My parents were looking at the suffering in their own life.

When a child gets told in a sentence with no explanation, "Your aunt was taken away", it means family is not a safe place to be in. When a child is left alone with the questions of what happened and how it happened, it is formative for life.

> I learned from the way my parents responded to the murder of Anna that a family is not a safe place to be. A family member can be taken away, without the consent of the family. The family cannot protect children.

Anna was only 29 years old when she died in the gas chamber. When I was her age, I was living in India seeking spiritual enlightenment. I was angry with my parents and could not understand how my father could serve in an army that was part of the regime that killed his sister. After years in India, I emigrated to the United States of America.

When I lived in the United States of America, I was lonely as a person. I was successful as an architect and clay artist but I was a foreigner in a country where "German" means good quality products, or it means living with the assumption that being "German" means being a Nazi. Yet there is a part of me which feels at home with being a stranger.

EMIGRATION

I make my HOME in foreign countries
When people ask me
I tell them I am from Germany
and they don't ask more
They are alone with Nazi
... or 'made in Germany'
and I am alone
not wanting to know
in my HOMELESSNESS

Sarva Posey

My response to the family secret when I was left with the sparse information about my aunt Anna was that I withdrew more and more from the family. I separated myself and went into inner emigration. As a child, I was a ferocious reader; by the age of eighteen I had left the family and moved to a different town, and by the age of 27, I left the country.

During the years I practiced architecture, I started working with clay as a way to express myself more freely and immediately. I recognized that my sculptures where influenced by architectural constructions and the culture I lived in, the process of doing it, itself was nebulous. It was only by becoming an expressive arts therapist many years later, which I was able to see the process as a way of gaining emotional access to my artworks. In my art I wanted a way to express what I could not express in words: the mysterious dark, the unspeakable, and my emotions. I liked using my hands to shape the material and how it felt on my skin, and I liked watching the movement of my hands. This process gave me insight into the artist-artwork relationship. McNiff states: "We have become accustomed to artists and therapists saying, 'Trust the process. Relax and follow its lead. Let it speak through you. Don't try and control it. Open to that which appears from outside your frame of reference'" (48). Making art was to balance my everyday life, especially the challenging work of an architect.

Creating Knowledge: Being in Relationship

To be a descendant of a Euthanasia victim is a commonality I share with the participants of this study. The common background in our families' history, the incomprehensible crime perpetrated on our family members helped create a trusting relationship between the participants and myself. The participants trusted me with the stories of their family and their own life stories because I was "one of them." They dedicated time to the interview, to phone conversations, and emails to provide information about their families. This trust gave me strength to continue even when the work was challenging. I felt a responsibility towards the participants to finish the research.

As a researcher, I am a witness to the lives of the descendants and to the stories. To rephrase Linden, I am representing the participants by way of the interviews (71) as the participants are representing the victims through publications and speaking about their family history publicly and among family members. Participants as researchers are giving voice to the victims, telling their life stories, and with these, their own story.

As Linden states, "I wanted to explore how knowledge is created, in and through conversation and introspection—knowledge that consists of moments of identification and understanding as well as impossible chasms and ruptures" (145).

I read this intriguing quote over and over again. Knowledge has a momentary existence—it is a mere flash in time. I would like to freeze this moment to examine it carefully, but it is impossible. At times I identify with the participants. There are similarities and intersections in our lives. I can comprehend the joys and sorrows we share in our daily lives. We create knowledge through being in relationship.

> Cleaning the "Stolpersteine"
> After lunch we drove to the town of Lahr. Gardy drives a nice car, a convertible. It is a hot sunny day and Gardy opens the sunroof of the car. She feels free when she drives the car, she tells me. Gardy brought her utensils to clean the fifteen "Stolpersteine" that are distributed around town. The memorials to the Holocaust and Euthanasia victims are small square brass plaques are embedded in the cobblestone and asphalt sidewalks of the streets.
> We stopped at the first memorial, two plaques laid side by side. The plaques are for a couple that died in the Holocaust. Gardy pulled out her gloves, a rag and the cleaning fluid. It was like a ritual. She put on the gloves and bent down to the street to clean the plaques. While Gardy cleaned the plaques, an older man and a young man who appeared to be his son came from the nearby café and asked what we were doing and what the stones stood for. Gardy told the two men the story of the plaques

while I asked them where they came from: They were Kurds from Turkey, an ethnic minority that is persecuted by the Turkish government.

While Gardy cleansed the second plaque in front of a jewelry store she told me the story of how the plaque was not welcome to the owner of the building. It had got lost during some street work and then replaced with a wrong name, but finally it is now the right plaque with the correct name of the Holocaust victim. This plaque is located at a busy pedestrian street. None of the passers-by seemed to notice us. The people just walked by ignoring the two women, one of them cleaning the "Stolpersteine."

The first plaque is dedicated to Gardy's grandmother. It is placed in front of the school her grandmother attended as a child. The young Kurdish boy whom we were talking to, attends the same school.

The next plaque is situated in front of a hairdresser's shop at a street intersection. There was no business on this hot afternoon and the young shop owners watched us without saying a word or inquiring what we were doing. I was holding the utensils and Gardy was cleaning the plaque. Trying to make contact with the couple, I asked if they knew the meaning of the plaque in front of their shop. In listening to their answer I heard from their speech that they were not native to Germany. First the man was very reluctant to tell me where he was from, and only said that they lived in a nearby town. When I insisted, he told me that they were originally from Serbia, a war-torn country.

While Gardy and I were approaching the last plaques to clean, a van from a charitable organization stopped in front of the house across the street. A little boy was being carried out from the car into his mother's arms, a child returning from the daycare facility for disabled children. A neighboring woman was standing by greeting the mother and the little boy. Gardy was cleaning the plaque and asked the woman if she knew what the it stood for. "I know what the plaque means," she said. She watched us for a bit, not saying anything and then we left.

Our last stop was in front of a house with five plaques. I took the rag and started cleaning. Gardy was sitting on a doorstep and remarked: "It is different now, I watch and you clean." Gardy cleans her fifteen memorials once a month.

The Names of the victims: Lilly Reckendorf, Caroline Maier, Carl Meier, Julie Haberer, Karl Haberer, Anneliese Pollak née. Lederer, Jenny Lederer née. Wertheimer, Leopold Lederer, Hans Herbert Lederer, Walter Lederer, Adolf Himmelsbach, Franz Ehinger, Ida Baumert, Karl Radlbeck, Katharina Viser.

Sensory Awareness, Visual Images

In my father's photo album I found a sepia-colored print of a family photo with Anna, her siblings, and her mother. The photo shows Anna as a child with my grandmother, my father Josef, and his little brother Ludwig. His little hands are clasped in front of him. Anna's sisters, Theresa and Maria, frame the group. My grandmother is wearing a black dress with a high collar. Her face is half in the shadow and looks very soft. Theresa stands on the left side of my grandmother looking towards the photographer. My father leans against his sister who seems to hold him. He stands in between his mother and Theresa with his hands touching both. His little suit with a white collar and cuffs on his tunic is made of the same material as the girl's dresses. The photo was taken in a studio with the silhouette of a landscape in the background.

Anna must have been about six years old. In the picture she is leaning against the shoulder of her mother very tenderly. Her hands are resting in the crook of her mothers' elbow. She is wearing a checkered dress with a white collar and a black bow like her sisters. The bow is holding her light brown, curled hair back from her face. She smiles and her face looks relaxed. As the only person in the photograph she is not looking at the photographer but seems to be looking inward. Anna's mouth is slightly open, and I wonder if it is an expression of her illness, the virus that destroyed the function of her brain. There is no photo of her as an adult.

This photo shows a family portrait, typical of this time, of a mother surrounded by her children. Yet the photo is unusually fluid in its composition with everybody touching each other. Each person is dressed in his or her Sunday finest. There is nothing in this picture which points to the death of Ludwig a few months later, or that Anna will die a violent death twenty-three years later. Four years after the photo was taken, Anna was ten years old; her father Josef Franz, who is not in the photograph, died. Her mother Maria died two years after her father's death. This family photo is both a document and an artwork. It conveys the impression that the people in the photo are close to each other and connected. I am proud to be part and a descendant of this family.

In writing about Anna, and I am also writing about the grandparents I never met. It is the first time in my life that I have thought about my grandparents, and I am almost sixty years old as I write this. I feel tenderness towards my grandmother surrounded by her children.

Using my imagination creates a feeling of closeness to my aunt Anna and her fate. She died in 1941, nine years before I was born. Through my research, Anna became alive in my imagination. Shedding light on her life makes her part of me. Embracing her in this way lifts the lid on the family secret and gives her a place in the family. Her life had a purpose. This purpose stands in contrast to Nazi ideology, which saw people with disability as not worth living. I submitted for entrance to the doctoral program at the European Graduate School a theater play in form of a dialog between Anna and myself which is based on the end of Anna's life in juxtaposition to my own life, In my research I used art-making both as a way to look at despair and as a way to struggle against it (Hermann 104-111).

> I am aware of the stark white walls and the high ceilings, my steps reverberating on the cold stone floor. Even though the place is washed in natural light, it exudes a coldness that reflects the atrocities that happened in this place. I feel vulnerable and self-conscious wearing colorful printed linen trousers and a yellow shirt. The height of the walls makes me feel small. There is nothing that puts me at ease in this place.
>
> My eyes are wide open and I absorb as many details as possible. I am aware of the rattle of a bunch of keys when the caretaker opens and looks the doors at the memorial site.

4.3.6 Conclusion of the Findings: LIFE Worthy of Life

After the introduction of the Euthanasia victims and their tragic destinies, I describe the participants from my observations (Glesne 44). In doing so, I honor the human story and get deep understandings of the issues pertaining to the themes of this study.

The findings show how the family secret gets passed onward. There can be a chasm between the generations and the people of the same generation in a family. The chasm is built by the taboo and being ashamed of the disabled family member. The chasm is also, to use a different metaphor, what Bar-On (33) depicted as a double wall between the generations. It is almost impossible to break the wall because both people have to be open at the same time. Time can widen the chasm as the atrocious crimes are forgotten.

In families where the violent death of the family member is disclosed and researched, the family members became closer and are able to face current conflicts and support each other. In some families, emotional closeness is momentary.

The quality of life is not necessary different from any other group of people in the beginning of the 21st century in Germany. Most of the participants are engaged in a social activity, adding *meaning to life*, with the awareness that there are people who are less fortunate and a desire to keep the memories of the victims alive. Some of the participants stated that being a descendant is only part of their heritage; otherwise, they enjoy life through art-making, crafts, physical activities, social life, and relaxation through entertainment and being in relationship.

The effect to the findings through decentering with art-making during the interview was that some of the answers deepened and new aspects to the issues in question were discovered. After the decentering and during the harvesting, the restated questions let the participants re-examine the answers. The participants were able to access emotions and show pride in their work. A surprise occurred in the moments of silence between aesthetic analysis and harvesting, unpleasant memories could surface and were spoken out; loneliness was faced with sometimes an opening up to the other family members.

In my role as researcher, I started with the vague feeling that my life and relationships were influenced by something which was beyond my control. Through the research into the life of my aunt Anna, I feel a responsibility for this heritage and keeping the memories of the Euthanasia victims alive. Throughout the study, I reflected on the copy with private vignettes to express my feelings of homelessness, emigration, and exclusion; and finally finding some consolidation. As a researcher, I gained knowledge through being in a trusting relationship with the participants.

5.0 RECOMMENDATIONS FOR FURTHER RESEARCH

5.1 Implications of This Study

The study explores the meaning of being a second or third generation descendant of a Nazi Euthanasia victim. As stated in the introduction of this study, the extent of the crimes with 275,000 victims touches on the lives of millions of families. I have provided a contextually sensitive set of personal narratives that productively expand theoretical and personal understanding of post trauma victimhood. According to Dr. Lilienthal, the original contact for this dissertation, this study is the first dissertation on the descendants of Euthanasia victims. To break through the secrecy and taboo concerning Euthanasia victims, decentering with art-making was used throughout the study both to deepen and expand the information shared by participants and to provide a container for my personal journey as a descendant.

One outcome of this study is a better understanding of the participants and of the implications of what it means to be a descendant of a Euthanasia victim—its shame and stigma.

There are institutions in which patients with hereditary epilepsy are living in the same institution where family members were Euthanasia victims. Second and third generation families of the Holocaust and scholars interested in their experience deserve to better understand the detailed and multifaceted layers of impact of secrets and shame related to these intersecting positions of marginality.

This study can contribute to a better understanding of more nuanced research strategies and further research into the lives of the descendants. This information can contribute to the educational work of the memorial sites and to further awareness among the general population, scholars, health care providers and family members of victims seeking to better understand this population.

5.2 Suggestions for Further Research

This study has shown the critical importance of further research that helps to identify the kinds of support needed for the descendants of this specific type of trauma. Other groups of descendants of crime victims also may be able to profit from this study. The methods and findings of this study may inspire related work with similar populations experiencing victimhood.

This study also opens the way to further studies using the arts in research. The arts seem particularly appropriate for issues that require understanding and respect for the multiple subjectivities inherent in exploring sensitive, personally and historically contextualized narratives. Using arts-based strategies could also expand to different settings and could employ multiple modalities for data collection, analysis and representation using intermodal expressive arts.

5.3 Further Aspirations

My hope in this study has been to contribute to changes in society that will increase public and private sensitivity to the issues explored and to help people to overcome their sense of victimhood. I hope that it is possible for the descendants of trauma to be able to support each other, to tell their stories as I have told mine and to bear witness to each other's stories with careful listening and decentering with the arts.

Sarva Posey, Life as Art, Mixed Media, 2001

BEARINGS AND VALUE

The positions are:
not to waste
demand respect
to control it all:
keep resentments

than again:
busy hands
enjoy the meaning of small things
care for loved ones
have time alone
to wage war against
victimhood
stem the black tied of depression

it is better already
and still challenging

Francine Guibentif and Sarva Posey

6.0 WORKS CITED

AKTION REINHARDT CAMPS. *Euthanasia*.Web. 05.Feb. 2012.
http://www.deathcamps.org/euthanasia/t4overview.html
APPALACHIAN EXPRESSIVE ARTS COLLECTIVE. *Expressive Arts Therapy: Creative Process in Art and Life*. Boone, N.C.: Parkway Publishers, 2003. Print.
BAR-ON, DAN. *Die Last des Schweigens, Gespräche mit Kindern von Nazi-Tätern*. Reinbek bei Hamburg: Rowohlt Taschenbuch Verlag, 1996. Print.
---. *The Bystander in Relation to the Victim and the Perpetrator; Today and During the Holocaust*. Ben Gurion University of the Negev, 2007. Print.
BINDING, KARL HOCHE, ALFRED. *Die Freigabe der Vernichtung lebensunwertem Lebens*. Berlin: Berlinger Wissenschafts-Verlag, 2006. Print.
CRESWELL, JOHN W. *Qualitative Inquiry & Research Design: Choosing Among Five Approaches*. Thousand Oaks: Sage Publications, 2007. Print.
CHÖDRÖN, PEMA. *When Things Fall Apart: Heart Advice for Difficult Times*. Boston: Shambala Publications, 1997. Print.
CLARK, KELLY. *Moving Beyond Recognition: Voices of Women Academics That Have Experience Being First-Generation College Students*. Diss. University of Vermont, Burlington, 1999. Print.
DELIUS, PETER. "Nationalsozialistische Gewaltmaßnahmen gegen psychisch Kranke: Bewältigungswege von Familienangehörigen." *Psychiatrische Praxis*. 18 (1991): 64-69. Print.
---. "Die psychisch kranken Opfer des Nationalsozialismus und ihre Familien." *Schleswig-Holsteinisches Ärzteblatt 3* (1992): 29-34. Print.
DENZIN, NORMAN & YVONNA LINCOLN. *Handbook of Qualitative Research* (2nd ed.). Thousand Oaks, CA: Sage, 2000. Print.
DÖRNER, KLAUS. *Tödliches Mitleid: Zur Frage der Unerträglichkeit des Lebens*. Gütersloh: Verlag Jakob van Hoddis, 1989. Print.
EBERHART, HERBERT, AND PAOLO J. KNILL. *Lösungskunst, Lehrbuch der Kunst- und ressourcenorientierten Arbeit*. Göttingen: Vandenhoeck & Ruprecht, 2009. Print.
ELLIS, CAROLYN. *The Ethnographic I: A Methodological Novel about Autoethnography*. Walnut Creek, CA: Alta Mira Press, 2004. Print.
FLEßNER, ALFRED. "NS-‚Euthanasie' im Land Oldenburg. Untersuchung von Erinnerungsarbeit und Geschichtsverarbeitung- Zwischenbericht eines zweijährigen Forschungsvorhabens." Arbeitskreis zur Erforschung der Nationalsozialistischen Euthanasie und Zwangssterilisation (Hrg): Tödliches Mitleid NS „Euthanasie" und Gegenwart. Berichte des Arbeitskreises, Band 4. Münster: Klemm & Oelschläger, 2007. Print.
GAY, LORRAINE & PETER AIRASIAN. *Educational Research: Competencies for Analysis and Application*. Upper Saddle River, NJ: Pearson Education, 2003. Print
Gedenkstätte Grafeneck, Dokumentationszentrum, Ausstellungsband "Euthanasie"-Verbrechen in Südwestdeutschland. Gedenkstätte Grafeneck, 2007. Print.
GEORGE, UTA ET AL. (EDS.). *Hadamar: Heilstätte, Tötungsanstalt, Therapiezentrum*. Marburg: Jonas Verlag, 2006. Print.

GLESNE, CORRINE. *Becoming Qualitative Researchers: An Introduction.* New York: Longman, 1999. Print.
GRUEN, ARNO. *Der Fremde in Uns.* Munich: Deutscher Taschenbuch Verlag, 2007. Print.
HERMAN, LISA. "Ethics and Imagination: Engaging Images of Evil in a Postmodern World." *Poesies: A Journal of Arts and Communication 3* (2002): 104-111. Print.
KLEE, ERNST. *'Euthanasie' im NS-Staat. Die Vernichtung lebensunwerten Lebens.* Frankfurt am Main: Fischer Taschenbuchverlag, 2009. Print.
KNEUKER, GERHARD, AND STEGLICH WULF. *Begegnungen mit der Euthanasie in Hadamar.* Rehburg-Loccum: Psychiatrie Verlag, 1985. Print.
KNILL, PAOLO, ELLEN G. LEVINE, AND STEPHEN K. LEVINE. *Principles and Practice of Expressive Arts Therapy: Towards a Therapeutic Aesthetics.* London: Kinsley, 2005. Print.
KORNFIELD, JACK. *The Wise Heart: A Guide to the Universal Teachings of Buddhist Psychology.* New York: Bantam Books, 2008. Print.
KRIZ, JÜRGEN. "Kritische Reflexion über Forschungsmethoden in den Künstlerischen Therapien." *Forschungsmethoden Künstlerischer Therapien.* Ed. Peter Petersen. Stuttgart: Mayer, 2002. Print.
LEAVY, PATRICIA. *Method Meets Art: Arts Based Research Practice.* New York: Guilford, 2009. Print.
LEVINE, STEPHEN. *Trauma, Tragedy, Therapy: The Arts and Human Suffering.* London: Jessica Kingsley, 2009. Print.
LINDEN, RUTH. *Making Stories, Making Selves: Feminist Reflections on the Holocaust.* Columbus: Ohio State UP, 1993. Print.
LIFTON, ROBERT JAY. *The Nazi Doctors: Medical Killing and the Psychology of Genocide.* Basic Books. 2000. Print.
McNIFF, SHAUN. *Art as Medicine: Creating a Therapy of the Imagination.* Boston: Shambala, 1992. Print.
MECKEL, MARLIS. *Den Opfern ihre Namen Zurückgeben.* Freiburg: Rombach, 2006. Print.
MITSCHERLICH, ALEXANDER, AND MARGARETE MITSCHERLICH. *Die Unfähigkeit zu trauern: Grundlagen kollektiven Verhaltens.* München. Piper Verlag, 2001. Print.
MUELLER-HOHAGEN, JÜRGEN. *Geschichte in uns: Seelische Auswirkungen bei den Nachkommen von NS-Tätern und Mitläufern.* Vol. 2. Dachau: Dachau Institut für Psychologie und Pädagogik, 2002. Print.
PATTON, MICHAEL. *Qualitative Research and Evaluation Methods.* Thousand Oaks, CA: Sage, 2002. Print.
PERNER, ROTRAUD A. *Darüber spricht man nicht: Tabus in der Familie.* München: Kösel Verlag, 1999. Print.
POSEY, SARVA LUCIA. "What motivates Non-Traditional Students to Study Late in Life?" pilot study, Appalachian State University, 2004. Print.
---. *Sinnes Erfahrungen mit – und in der Natur: Ein intermodaler Ansatz in der Kunst- und Ausdruckstherapie.* Ed. Ruth Hampe, Peter Stalder. Berlin: Frank &Timme Verlag, 2011. Print.
RICHARDS, M.C. *The Fire Within.* Kane-Lewis Production, 2003. DVD.

RICHTER, GABRIEL, ED. *Die Fahrt ins Graue(n): Die Heil-und Pflegeanstalt Emmendingen 1933-1945 und danach*. Emmendingen: Druckerei Kesselring, 2005. Print.

RUDER, GARDY-KÄTHE. "Euthanasie im Nationalsozialismus." Kippenheim. 26 Nov. 2000. Lecture.

---. *Holocaust im Gedächtnis einer Puppe*. Baden-Baden: Deutscher Wissenschafts-Verlag, 2006. Print.

SCHNEIDER, BEATE. "Nachforschungen zum Tod meiner Großtante Karoline F." An-dernach, 27 Jan. 2009. Lecture and PowerPoint.

SCHNEIDER, BEATE. *Nassauische Neue Presse*. "Gedenkfeier: Angehörige forschen nach den Lebens-und Leidensgeschichten." 16 Jan. 2007. Print.

STAKE, ROBERT E. *Multiple Case Study Analysis*. New York: Guilford, 2006. Print.

ST. PIERRE, ELIZABETH. "Decentering Voice in Qualitative Inquiry." *International Review of Qualitative Research*. 1.3 (2008): 319-336. Print.

TIEDEMANN, JENS. *Die Intersubjektive Natur der Scham*. Diss. University of Berlin, 2007. Print.

VAN MAANEN, JOHN. *Tales of the Field: On Writing Ethnography*. Chicago: Chicago UP, 1988. Print.

VOLKAN, VAMIK, D., GABRIELE AST, AND WILLIAM F. GREER, JR. *The Third Reich in the Unconscious: Transgenerational Transmission and its Consequences*. New York: Brunner-Routledge, 2002. Print.

VON GLASERSFELD, ERNST. "An Introduction to Radical Constructivism." From (Ed.) P. WATZLAWICK. *The Invented Reality*. New York: Norton. 1984. Web. n.d.

WILLIAMS, MARK, J. TEASDALE, Z. SEGAL, AND J. KABAT-ZINN. *The Mindful Way through Depression: Freeing Yourself from Chronic Unhappiness*. New York: Guilford, 2007. Print.

WOLCOTT, HARRY F. *Transforming Qualitative Data: Description, Analysis, and Interpretation*. Thousand Oaks, CA: Sage, 1994. Print.

YOW, MELISSA. *Recording Oral History: A Practical Guide for Social Sciences*. New York: Rowman & Littlefield, 2004. Print.

ZUMTHOR, PETER. *Thinking Architecture*. Basel: Birkhäuser, 1998. Print.

7.0 APPENDIX

7.1 Lay Summary

Breaking the wall of shame

An ethnographic study with descendants of Euthanasia victims of Nazi Germany, and a dissertation in the English language at the European Graduate School, Leukstadt, Switzerland. Supervision: Prof. Sally Atkins EdD, Appalachian State University, Boone, NC, USA, and European Graduate School

The lives of the descendants and family members of Euthanasia victims are depicted with the help of interviews and art-making. The study describes how the descendants see themselves and in relationships. It describes how they experience the unspoken in the family. This study is intended to give the descendants a voice and to keep the memory of the past alive. In contrast to other groups of Holocaust victims, the Euthanasia murders of patients and the consequences for their descendants have been little researched. The victims are not recognized as victims of the Holocaust.

During the interview (90 minutes), family members of the second and third generation tell their stories. Artistic activities are part of the interview (twenty minutes). This creative activity is one of the methods used in Expressive Arts Therapy and is embedded in the interview. After the art-making phase, the questions are repeated in order to reflect on the themes of the interview again.

As a researcher, I am also an artist and ethnographer. As an artist, I express how I am personally affected by making art. I reflect on my experiences using creative activities. I also look at this study with the eyes of an Expressive Arts Therapist. Creative activity (in art therapy) is psychotherapy with artistic methods. It is a method where people tell their story and how it affects them. I am a family member of a Euthanasia victim and my family is also affected by and involved in this study.

Lucia Posey   November 2008
Expressive Arts Therapist M.A., Ph.D. cand.
Art therapist DGKT

7.2 A Dialog between Anna and Lucy

The stage:
A large abstract painting serves as a backdrop, otherwise the stage is empty, except for a wooden bench.

The cast:
Anna: a young twenty nine-year-old woman is living in the psychiatric hospital since twenty years. It is the year 1941.
Lucy: Her middle-aged niece, looking back over the last forty years.

Anna is sitting on a wooden bench. It is February 13, 1941, a cold but sunny afternoon. She is wrapped in a dark gray winter coat. It is a coarse men's wool coat, a hand out from the hospital. Her brown hair is cut short and the wind is playing with the few curly ends. Her hands are buried in the coat pockets, her shoulders pulled up. Sometimes she turns her head and looks at the sun, and then her head drops again, falling down on her chest. Her crossed legs are covered in brown hand knitted wool stockings and she is wearing black-laced winter boots. Anna, speaks haltingly with a small slow voice, the words are blurred:

"I live in this big old building with my friends, Leni and Franz and ..."

She smiles and makes an uncertain gesture with her hand.

Pause

Lucy enters the stage. She is wearing a dark blue coat out of a cashmere wool mix. It is from an expensive department store. She stands at some distance from Anna. Lucy starts to recite a poem. As she starts talking she takes off her coat and let it fall on the floor.

DARK BLUE COAT

leaves of autumn
slowly sailing
to the soft green bed
white hair
on my dark blue coat
tree trunks, pale grey bones
show beneath
the lush green summer garments
like the ageing body
beneath the dark blue coat.

Sarva Posey

2.13.1941, Anna:
"I am here living in this big house since a long time. I get so confused and mix up things. Mom and dad brought me here. It is a long time ago, I remember, she waived good-bye. She was ill too, and so was dad. We really didn't have enough to eat at home."

1961 Lucy:
"I am eleven years old, and Nanny, my aunt, just died unexpectedly. Nanny took care of me and had her own troubles, leaving me an orphan. I am in the kitchen with the old yellow cupboard and the sugar tin. I am bored and lonely, knowing if I left the house I will get recruited to work in the plant nursery. My lonelyness makes me want to eat pieces of dark heavy bread with the hard crust. I can feel the crunch of the white sugar on a thick layer of cool yellow butter.

2.13.1941, Anna:
"I ask dad where mama is, she is working at the store, he said, that is why she is not in the photograph."

1963 Lucy:
"I am thirteen years old and I just started dieting, having gained much weight in the last two years, since Nanny died. My body changed and I started bleeding every month. Suddenly I feel attracted to boys and think about how I look. I just started dieting like they said in the women's magazine I secretly read. I didn't eat food I ate eight hundred calories a day. Twiggy was the ideal. I wanted to look like

her in the XS dress, loosely falling from my shoulders, maybe then I will be loved by a luscious, sensuous longhaired John Lennon hippie, white lacy shirt and gold chains around his neck, me his "Lucy in the sky with diamonds."

Anna is teary eyed.

2.13.1941 Anna:
"Where are Maria, Resi and Josef, my sisters and brother?"

Pause

"I miss them. We were sitting all together in the little cart and dad was pulling us. I have not seen them for a long time. They did not visit me."

2004 Lucy:
"I never really stopped worrying about food and my body. I look in the mirror every morning and hope that I lost a pound, despite the Ben and Jerry's ice cream I ate the night before. I am concerned when I go clothes shopping. It's about the size L in the label. I am thrilled if I manage an M, where it used to be S and petite. I don't buy an XL; I rather leave the unfriendly changing cabin with the glaring neon lights, sweaty, feeling old. It's been a rollercoaster really, up and down with the weight all my life."

2.13.1941:
Two big grey busses are pulling into the courtyard, we hear the noise of their engines.

Anna looks at Lucy.

"They just called me to come and get on the bus. We are leaving."

Anna gets up from the bench and goes off the stage. Her right foot is dragging behind and her right arm is hanging limp on her side.

2005 Lucy:
bending down picking up her coat.
"I am an older single woman, pulling back into the anonymity of the overweight body and the eyeglasses. It is not anymore the grey and white hair, but the pants and sweaters - which are already a few years old; not the pink and lime green fashion colors of this spring. It is the age of the rubber band waists and the shoe

insoles. The stiff and numb fingers and the aching ankles make it slow rising from the bed in the morning. It can happen any time, sitting at a table that the heat waves, like shame flooding my body."

She exits to the other side of the stage.